the Old Men

*The conversations that
help boys become men.*

T.L. Jones

Dedication

With all the love within me,
this book is dedicated to my children:

Benjamin Jones, Hannah Barnes, and Lydia Price.

4

Acknowledgements

The first person to suggest that I put some of my thoughts into book form was my wife, Martha Jones. She has always believed in me. I should've listened to her years ago.

Many people have encouraged me to write, and I'm thankful to each of them. Among the most persistent were my friends Tom Hatley, Jason McNeese, Dwight Smith, and Alton Beal. If this book finds any success, it will be in part due to their encouragement in the matter.

The real work of proof reading and editing this was done primarily by my friends Dwight and Amber Smith. They were assisted by Thomas Simpson. I simply could not have accomplished the final product without their help.

Forward

On a rare occasion, one finds a book that has a simply stated combination of wit, common sense, and wisdom, all in one place. This book is such a find. In the following pages, T.L. Jones will give his readers a treasured glimpse of the Appalachian Mountain ways he grew up learning.

Yet he has not simply written to reveal a slice of Americana. He has done so with a specific target in mind: Men. This group has been under attack for centuries, but it seems that recently, this assault has only intensified. This author, in his own wise and winsome way, offers a solution and counterattack to this affront to manhood – respect for the old men, their ways, and the lessons they have tried to convey to the generations that follow.

By example, T.L. Jones presents several short essays based upon specific truths the old men in his life have taught him. Each one is undergirded with a practical and helpful Bible verse that relates. Each one will thrill you. Each one will cause you to reflect upon your own duty to listen for the truths passed on by the old men in your life, to apply them, and to pass them down to the next generation.

In a day of such disrespect and disregard for the older generation, you will find these pages refreshing, compelling and challenging. It is my honor to present to you, "The Old Men" and the author, T.L. Jones.

Dwight Smith

Table of Contents

Introduction

"If just one generation would learn from the previous generation, what a difference it would make."
Dad

O ne of the greatest advantages of life is growing up with old men who care about you and your future. They are a treasure trove of wisdom, knowledge and skill. I've been fortunate enough to have a dad, a papaw and many other old men who invested into my life from birth. My life has been blessed beyond description, in countless ways, due to my relationship with them.

As a boy, I wasn't really aware of the lifelong benefits I was receiving from them in everyday life. When I was in my early twenties, my dad said to me, *"If just one generation would learn from the previous generation, what a difference it would make."* That statement became a bedrock principle of my life. As I meditated on that thought, I determined that I would stop living the hard way and start trying, by the grace of God, to learn from the wisdom and experiences of others as much as I could.

Experience is often said to be the best teacher, but I have often found experience to be a cruel and merciless teacher that gives the test first and the lesson second. The best way to learn is to soak up the generational wisdom of others. Boys especially need to learn from old men. The casual conversations that happen between old men and boys as they live, work and play together is essential to boys becoming men. When an old man shares his wisdom with a boy, and that boy receives that wisdom, the boy is getting more than what that one man has learned. *He is getting what multiplied generations have handed down through the centuries.* In this way, thousands of years of manly wisdom and skill are passed from one generation to the next. The entire book of Proverbs is based on this principle. It reveals an older man seeking to train his son to navigate life with generational wisdom given by God through the old men.

This book contains eighty-four essays where I share with the reader what my old men shared with me. Their words have helped me every step of the way and saved me a great deal of unnecessary pain. As you read the essays, my hope is that you will see the wisdom of walking with God and learning from old men. Hopefully, the lessons I was taught will help you directly and bring to remembrance the valuable truths your old men taught you. *This is the way of boys becoming men.* There is no generation gap between old men who care for their boys and boys who respect their old men.

Peace be with you,

T.L. Jones

> *"Thou shalt rise up before the hoary head,*
> *and honour the face of the old man, and fear*
> *thy God: I am the LORD" (Leviticus 19:32).*

1

Poppy's Shoulders

"One day while I was at school, it came a snow, and Poppy had to walk to the school to get me. He put me on his shoulders and carried me all the way home."
Berry Tarlton (Papaw)

In our culture, our elders are revered and shown the honor they deserve by those they brought into this world. In the mountains of southern Appalachia, we call our grandfathers "Papaw."* A good Papaw is a gift from God, and mine was top of the line. If Papaws were metal, mine was pure gold. I spent a large portion of my childhood with mine – farming, hunting, and "loafering."

Papaw was one of my old men. The moniker "old man" in our mountains isn't degrading or demeaning. It means you've lived long enough for the next generation to view you as an elder and to show you proper respect. These old men taught us by word and example the things we needed to know in life to navigate the real world. Sometimes they were rough around the edges. Their words didn't always come wrapped in velvet and lace. Other times they said nearly nothing but expected you to learn through observation. They almost never gave lectures. They spoke and simply moved on. This is the way of wisdom among men. *The old men speak, and the young men listen.*

My Papaw referred to his dad as "Poppy." Poppy was a mountain man that had taken care of a large family by working a mountain farm. Today, people want mountain land because it's beautiful, but when this area was settled by Europeans, the mountain land was taken by poor people who couldn't afford river bottom land. To survive in the mountains, you had to work hard and live on very little. It made tough men, the kind of men who won WWI and WWII.

Papaw and I were riding around one day, when we passed an old school building that had been unoccupied and rotting down my entire life. He told me that's where he went to school as a small boy. Papaw said, *"One day while I was at school, it came a snow, and Poppy had to walk to the school to get me. He put me on his shoulders and carried me all the way home."* That walk, in the deep snow, with his son on his back, is what this book is about.

The old school were Poppy carried Berry home from in the snow.
Located in Houston Valley (Greene County, TN).

Old men have a responsibility to carry their sons on their shoulders until their sons can make that walk with their own full-grown legs. Boys need old men. They need their words. They need their strength. They need their example. The old men help the boys become men every day, by just being men in front of them.

"Children's children are the crown of old men; and the glory of children are their fathers" (Proverbs 17:6).

*"Pa" is pronounced like "pa" in the word "past." "Paw" is pronounced the same way you refer to a dog's paw.

Spencer Tarlton (Poppy).

2

Follow the Compass

"You go whichever way you want to go, but I'm going to follow this compass out of here."
Terry Jones (Dad)

The men in my family were big game hunters. Primarily they bear hunted with hounds. If you ever visit East Tennessee and wander off into some of our laurel-infested ridges, you'll understand that chasing bears in our country isn't for the weak at heart. The bear hunters knew the mountains like the back of their hands and needed no navigational tools but their own experience to get anywhere and out of anywhere. Getting lost was just not something that happened often or ever.

Everything was different in the spring, however, when they took their annual trip to Canada. The topography of Ontario was flat and swampy. Without mountain peaks to give them a frame of reference, they could go round and round and get nowhere. Getting lost in thousands of acres of roadless Canadian swamp is deadly. In the spring, just the flies and gnats are enough to drive you insane.

To compensate for their lack of experience in the Canadian swamps, they carried maps and a compass. The East Tennessee bear hunters were sophisticated in the way they navigated with the tools. They simply found themselves on the map and determined which direction they would need to go to get back to the road where they parked their trucks. They might have come out on the highway a few miles away, but that was better than being endlessly lost.

On one particular trip, Dad and a hunting partner had launched into the wilderness from a railroad track that ran north and south. They went into the wilderness heading west, so all they had to do was go east to get back to the tracks when the hunt was over. Following hounds isn't like most hunting methods. Wherever the bear goes, the dogs go, and the hunters must follow no matter how deep or how rough it is. This way of hunting can put you into some real predicaments. Such was the case for Dad and his hunting partner.

They had gotten so far into the wilderness that they lost their sense of direction. Dad pulled out his compass and let it tell him which direction was east. This would absolutely put them back on the railroad tracks at some point. His hunting partner got it in his head that the compass was wrong and wanted to go the opposite direction. Dad told him, *"You go whichever way you want to go, but I'm going to follow this compass out of here."* Of course, the compass was right, and Dad and his reluctant partner safely made their way to the tracks.

Life requires a compass. It requires a navigation tool that's absolute in its bearings. For me that navigation tool is the Bible. I have found it to be 100% reliable in getting me through the maze of life. The only way to get to where you want to go is to go in the right direction. Simply follow the compass.

"As for God, his way is perfect: the word of the LORD is tried: he is a buckler to all those that trust in him" (Psalm 18:30).

The author's father, Terry Jones.

Stop Looking Behind You

"Every time you look behind you – you lose a step."
Wade Erwin

W ade Erwin was my favorite teacher in the public school system. He was a friend of my dad's and a bear hunter himself. He understood us mountain boys and knew how to communicate with us. He was my 5th grade teacher which also included Physical Education. After school he was the elementary school football coach.

I have no idea of Mr. Erwin's personal athletic accomplishments. He never spoke of them to us. His focus was always on the task at hand and how to coach us to be successful at the given task.

In PE class we did all sorts of things from basketball to folk dancing. Part of our exercise included running laps around the gym. Mr. Erwin would watch us as we ran. One thing that bothered him specifically was catching a runner looking behind them. He'd yell, *"Every time you look behind you – you lose a step."* He wanted our eyes fixed forward. He wanted us to make every step count as we ran.

Lots of folks in life struggle to make forward progress because they are too fixated on their past. They're always looking in the rearview mirror and not at the road in front of them. They're troubled by past sins. Mistakes, made long ago, are shackles to them. The only hope for them is to stop looking over their shoulder and look ahead. Mr. Erwin was right. Looking behind you is a losing effort.

"Brethren, I count not myself to have apprehended: but this one thing I do, forgetting those things which are behind, and reaching forth unto those things which are before" (Philippians 3:13).

Football Coach Wade Erwin

Piece of Junk Truck

"I wouldn't buy that truck. It's a piece of junk."
Dad

W hen I turned 16, in 1986, I had one thing on my mind. I wanted a 4x4 vehicle so I could hit the roads. My parents were both in favor of me getting a vehicle so that wasn't a problem. In fact, Dad offered to give me a 1974 Pontiac Lemans GT that my mom had driven for years. It was a great car and in immaculate condition. Best of all it was free, but I refused it because I wanted a 4x4 so I could hunt out of it. Dad had a 4x4 truck and a 4x4 Bronco which I could've used to hunt out of, but I wanted my own.

My only hold up was my budget. I had a grand total of $1500 and no job outside of helping on Papaw's farm. So, buying a 4x4 was going to empty my bank account, cause me to get a regular job, and take out a loan. That's a pretty big step for a junior in high school, but I was going to do it if it meant I could have my own 4x4.

I took a while, but I finally found a 1981 Nissan truck that I really wanted. So, I asked Dad to go look at it with me. Dad was a pretty good mechanic and a solid judge of used vehicles. He knew what to look for and what to stay away from. After looking it over Dad said, *"I wouldn't buy that truck. It's a piece of junk."* It had some after-market additions that Dad assumed had been installed by someone who didn't know what they were doing.

It was at this juncture I decided that I wanted the truck more than I wanted Dad's opinion. He was adamantly against it, but I made arrangements to buy the truck in spite of his advice. It was a terrible mistake!

That truck turned out to be a piece of junk just like Dad predicted. It left me stranded more than once, caught on fire once, and was a general headache as long as I owned it. The worst part was having to wash dishes at a restaurant to pay for it. My freedom was sacrificed to pay for a truck that I eventually hated. Wisdom and experience beat ignorance every time. Boys need Dads.

"My son, attend to my words; incline thine ear unto my sayings" (Proverbs 4:20).

The Junk Truck.

Can I Have a Cigarette?

*"I'll give you a cigarette, but if you
can't smoke the whole thing..."*
Dad

My Dad was a good, decent, honest, hardworking man, but he wasn't perfect. He knew his faults. We knew his faults. As a dad, he had the responsibility to raise me, and that meant modifying my behavior where he saw fit, in spite of his own imperfections.

One issue we had conflict over started much earlier than it should have. When I was about five, I asked Dad for a cigarette. I didn't know it at the time, but I think this question hit Dad right where it hurt. You see, he spent years and years of his life wanting to quit smoking but failed again and again.

When his little boy looked up into his face and asked for a cigarette, I think he realized that his failures and habits were potentially going to become mine and much earlier than he expected. Dad responded to my request in a way that I now look back on with much respect. He said, *"I'll give you a cigarette, but if you can't smoke the whole thing, I better never catch you with another one, or I'll bust your hind end."* I agreed. A few puffs into that cigarette and I was done. I couldn't stand it! It looked cool but was nasty to me. He took the cigarette from me and reminded me of our agreement. Dad always kept his word to me, so I knew what would happen if I ever touched one again.

Not long after that ordeal we had some company at the house, and we were just goofing off. Dad said he needed to run to the store, and he left me in the care of an adult cousin. My cousin asked me if I wanted a cigarette. I refused, knowing that Dad would make good on his deal. My cousin persisted and promised to protect me from Dad. Stupidly, I took the cigarette.

Dad rolled in just after I started puffing that thing and got out of the car. He walked up on the porch without saying a word. He took me by the arm, and we went into the house together. He applied the belt of education to my seat of knowledge. It was a lesson I've never forgotten.

I grew up knowing Dad smoked, and at the same time wouldn't allow me to smoke under a clearly defined penalty. Never once did I think of my dad as a hypocrite. He was an extremely strong man, but he wasn't strong enough to beat nicotine addiction. Cigarettes controlled him. He understood their power over him and simply didn't want me to have the same problem. That's not hypocrisy.

That's a dad knowing his own failures and desperately wanting his son to do better. Parents are not perfect. They struggle with various problems and weaknesses. The good ones want better for their kids even when they are underwater themselves.

If you're really smart, you'll try to learn both from your parents' strengths and weaknesses. Just for the record, Dad later told me that he would quit, and he finally did. I wasn't surprised that he kicked the habit because once he gave his word, he kept it.

"My son, hear the instruction of thy father, and forsake not the law of thy mother" (Proverbs 1:8).

Herd Mentality

"If you put a five-gallon bucket in the middle of the Asheville Highway and start running around it, it won't be long until other people start running around it with you."

Dad

If you gave my dad good advice, he would take it. He wasn't too prideful to listen to others with better ideas, but he wasn't one to follow others blindly. He was an independent thinker, and whatever decision he made would be of his own choosing.

In a discussion about religion, he said to me, *"If you put a five-gallon bucket in the middle of the Asheville Highway and start running around it, it won't be long until other people start running around it with you."* That's truer than I'd like it to be. Even relatively rational people get sucked into the herd mentality. Children need this explained to them early and often. Just because a large crowd is doing something doesn't mean it's a good idea to follow.

Life is better if you seek wise counsel. Life is better if you apply wise counsel. Ultimately, you absolutely must learn to think for yourself. Bad company will ruin you. Being sucked into a herd going the wrong direction has destroyed many lives in the religious, political and social aspects of life. Take responsibility for your own mind, your own thoughts and your own decisions. It's better to walk alone than to walk with a herd headed for a cliff.

"But the chief priests and elders persuaded the multitude that they should ask Barabbas and destroy Jesus" (Matthew 27:20).

Bad Company

*"The first Bible verse I ever taught
my son was Proverbs 1:10."*
Dr. John Godfrey (Pastor)

When I finished college, I was hired by Great Hope Baptist Church in Chesapeake, VA, to be their youth pastor. The senior pastor of that church was a marvelous man named John Godfrey. Pastor Godfrey was not only a great pastor but was a five-star family man. He loved his wife and children on purpose, and it was obvious.

When I got to Great Hope, Pastor Godfrey's son was in the 8th grade. Even at that young age he had already developed a heart for God. As a young Dad myself, I was open to any advice Pastor Godfrey had to offer concerning his relationship with his children. During one of our many discussions Pastor Godfrey said to me, *"The first Bible verse I ever taught my son was Proverbs 1:10."*

There are 31,102 verses in the Bible. It's no accident that a man as serious about his family as Pastor Godfrey chose this verse to be the first verse taught to his son. In Proverbs 1:10, Solomon, who is considered to be one of the wisest men to ever live, warns his son to reject the enticement of sinners. Bad company is a life destroyer. Psalm 1:1 teaches that living a blessed life requires one to avoid bad company and their advice. How many men are in prison right now because of bad company? How many boys went to premature graves because of wicked friends? Choose wisely who you let influence you.

"My son, if sinners entice thee, consent thou not" Proverbs 1:10).

Pastor John Godfrey

Making Much of Jesus

"Make much of Jesus, and He will make much of you."
Dr. Jerry Mullendore (Pastor)

My teen years were basically wasted on foolishness. God was merciful to me, and, at the age of 18, I became a Christian. Many people helped me in the early years of my Christian life – none more than Dr. Jerry Mullendore. He pastored Eastside Baptist Church in Greeneville, Tennessee. I first met him on a special Sunday that I attended with my Papaw who had been invited to share his testimony.

Pastor Mullendore helped me in more ways than I can count. Mostly, he was willing to spend hours just talking to me about the questions I had and giving me sound answers. He often said, from the pulpit, *"Make much of Jesus, and He will make much of you."* I don't think that quote originated with Pastor Mullendore, but he was the man that said it enough to make an impact on my life.

Jesus isn't just important. Jesus is life! He is the way to eternal life, and He's the source of abundant life on this side of eternity. My childhood wasn't focused on Jesus. My teen years were nearly entirely devoid of Jesus. Becoming a Christian was the best thing that ever happened to me! Everything good in my life is because of Jesus.

Jesus gave me eternal life. Jesus gave me purpose. Jesus gave me a fabulous wife. Jesus has given me awesome children and grandchildren. Jesus has provided every need I've ever had. He's never failed me!

Without Jesus I don't think I would have lived much longer past eighteen. Without Jesus, I certainly wouldn't have had a purpose to life-no meaning at all. When my focus is on Jesus, life makes sense to me. I do not claim I've been a great follower, but I do claim He's been a great Master. Dr. Mullendore was right. If you'll make much of Jesus, He'll make much of you. Boys need old men. They especially need old men who make much of Jesus.

"For to me to live is Christ, and to die is gain"
(Philippians 1:21).

36

Get Your Hands Out of Your Pockets

"Get your hands out of your pockets while we're trying to work."
Papaw

Papaw was a busy man. He worked a full-time factory job at Pet Milk. He ran a sixty-seven-acre farm which had cattle, hogs, hay, and tobacco. He was an elected Tennessee constable, which was a law enforcement officer. On top of that he had an apple orchard, kept honeybees and bear hunted. Except for watching the nightly news and sleeping, he seldom stopped. The only day with any significant rest was Sunday afternoon when he may sit a spell on the porch and talk to family and friends or take a walk through the mountains.

He never gave me a lecture about the importance of time. No lecture was necessary. If you were with him, you'd be doing something. One of his pet peeves was people who put their hands in their pockets when they were supposed to be working, and more than once he barked at me, saying, *"Get your hands out of your pockets while we're trying to work."*

Every time you put your hands in your pockets you have committed to not working for at least as long as it takes you to get your hands out of your pockets. Let's say the in and out process takes you one minute, and you do it 5 times an hour. That's over a half hour of wasted time in an 8-hour workday. In Papaw's generation that kind of waste would get you fired at the local factory, because plenty more men wanted that job who would work that half hour. Unless it was extremely cold, old man equated having your hands in your pockets as laziness.

> *"I must work the works of him that sent me, while it is day: the night cometh, when no man can work" (John 9:4).*

Bullying and Bullies

"If I hear that you've bullied some kid, I'll whip you when you get home. If I hear that you've allowed someone to bully, and you don't fight back, I'll whip you when you get home."

Dad

One of the earliest memories I have of Dad teaching me anything was when he taught me on the subject of bullying. Just before I started kindergarten Dad told me very clearly, *"If I hear that you've bullied some kid, I'll whip you when you get home. If I hear that you've allowed someone to bully, and you don't fight back, I'll whip you when you get home."* He wasn't joking, and I knew it. There was no discussion about "what ifs". Dad had laid down the rules about bullying and bullies and left me to follow his rules.

Dad didn't think much of people who had "loud mouths". Nor did he care for what he called "blow hards." He had a great deal of respect for people who would fight if they had to fight. He grew up without a present Dad, and I reckon he had to fend for himself on occasion. I never saw Dad pick a fight, and I never saw him express any fear of anyone either. He didn't want his son causing trouble. And he didn't want his son backing down from any either.

Jesus taught that Christians should "turn the other cheek". This is reference to an insulting but physically harmless slap. Turning the other cheek is not in reference to physically dangerous situations of bodily harm or potential death. There's nothing wrong with self-defense. This is basically what Dad taught me, even though he offered no Biblical insight on the matter. Dad was right about bullying and bullies. God doesn't make you strong so that you can harm the weak. However, if children can't defend themselves from dangerous bullies, the bullying will only get worse. Parents can't be with their children every minute of every day. Boys ought to be taught to defend themselves and have the green light to do it. Our sons need to be taught to seek peace and be prepared for war. We live in a dangerous world.

"Blessed be the LORD my strength, which teacheth my hands to war, and my fingers to fight" (Psalm 144:1).

11

Hills to Die On

*"You've got to decide which hills
you are willing to die on."*
Dr. John Halsey (Pastor)

In 1999, my family and I moved to Whitehall, Montana, to start a church. In June of that year, we held our first service, and little by little, the church gained numbers in attendance. It was my first pastorate. I quickly learned that there was a huge difference between being a youth pastor and being a senior pastor. About a month into the newly formed church, I joked with a friend of mine that leadership wasn't all it was cracked up to be.

I wasn't having problems with the clear doctrine of Scripture. Bible doctrine isn't up for grabs with me. My trouble was trying to make subjective judgments about how to pastor the church on issues where honest differences of opinion existed. Some pastors I knew took really hard lines on certain areas that other pastors didn't. In my heart I wanted to do the right thing in doctrine and in the application of Scripture. I was struggling, and if I'm completely honest, I was allowing the opinions of others too much influence in my thinking.

Dr. Halsey came to Montana to hold a special meeting for us focused on missions. I shared some of my struggles with him. He gave me a piece of advice that became a cornerstone of my pastoral philosophy. I credit his advice with possibly saving my ministry from a certain type of man-centered paralysis. He said, *"You've got to decide which hills you are willing to die on. If you're not willing to die on a hill, don't make it a hill."* That advice was life-altering for me as a young pastor.

Dr. Halsey was telling me to critically evaluate my decisions and determine their genuine importance in relation to the Word of God. If it was important enough to die for, it was worth any complications or reactions that might accompany it. If something wasn't truly important, then don't assign it importance. Something doesn't have to be a life-or-death matter to be important, but I was allowing unimportant matters to consume my life. Over the years I've tried to place everything into its proper category. Part of what's wrong with so many people today is that they make important things unimportant. And they make unimportant things important.

My son once told me that he was in a precarious situation, and this statement from Dr. Halsey came to his mind at a critical moment. He said that it led him to not do something that could've had negative consequences for his life. *The old man not only helped me, he also helped my son many years later.* Learn to decide what's important. Live like it's important.

"Ye blind guides, which strain at a gnat, and swallow a camel" (Matthew 23:24).

12

Talk Less

"Stay off the radio, and you'll kill more bear"
Dad

When a bear is running from hounds, he can cover a lot of ground fast. If your goal is to kill a bear being chased by hounds, you'll have to cover some ground yourself. Sometimes the difference between a successful hunt and a failed hunt is a split second.

The hunters that I grew up with communicated with one another using handheld walkie talkies they simply called radios. In the 1970's-80's those radios were much larger than they are now. My Dad cut the leg out of a pair of blue jeans and made a case for his radio with a sewn-on strap he hung over his shoulder. Their trucks were also equipped with CB's just like truckers used up and down the interstates. Some bear hunters were better at talking than they were killing bear.

Dad was a man of few words in everyday life and was exceptionally quiet while hunting. It frustrated him that men who were supposed to be helping kill a bear would be talking on the radio when they needed to be covering ground. He told me,

"Stay off the radio, and you'll kill more bear." Talk is cheap. Action is platinum in the bear woods. As I have gotten older, the less I care to talk. I've learned if you will say less and talk quieter that people actually listen to you more intently.

Talking less is actually Biblical in a lot of ways. It will certainly assist you in not saying things you shouldn't, and purposely talking less will help you to choose your words more carefully. Some aspects of life require verbal communication; however, most of us talk too much about too little. It hinders real productivity.

Dad was a proficient bear hunter. One of the reasons he killed bear when others didn't is because he was covering ground while they were talking about it. When an old man doesn't say much, I really want to hear what he does say.

"Be not rash with thy mouth, and let not thine heart be hasty to utter any thing before God: for God is in heaven, and thou upon earth: therefore let thy words be few" (Ecclesiastes 5:2).

Terry Jones with Hector - his favorite bear dog.

13

Kids Never Forget

*"He drove off and left me standing
there in the parking lot."*
Dad

One of the saddest stories Dad ever told me involved little league baseball. That's sort of ironic for me because baseball is my favorite sport, and my memories of little league baseball are nearly all good. The time of life that a boy plays little league ought to be the happiest time of his life.

Unfortunately for Dad, his experience with little league baseball turned sour one afternoon because of a man who had stronger views than his compassion could direct. Dad was raised by his mom who had to go it alone. Her husband had forsaken her and their four children when my dad was only two. During that time period, Grandmother's separation from her husband carried some strong negative feelings in the heart of a man in the community. That man's feelings would impact Dad for the rest of his life.

Dad was ready for baseball season to begin and wanted to get to practice. Not every family had a way for the kids to get to the baseball field, so several boys who needed a ride would meet at a community church, and one of the men would haul them to practice. Dad needed a ride too, so he went to the church at the designated time, expecting to be welcomed. He wasn't.

The man with the car didn't like my grandmother and her husband being separated. Somehow in his mind that made my dad socially unacceptable. He didn't want a boy who came from a home of separation to be in the car with the other boys from "good homes." That man, who identified as a Christian, refused to allow little Terry Jones, who had no dad, into his car, and drove off leaving Dad standing in the parking lot alone. No matter what you think the Bible teaches about divorce, in no way would Jesus lead a full-grown man to treat a child so heartlessly.

Dad didn't express any bitterness toward that man when he told me the story. He still seemed bewildered by the man's actions years later. He had never forgotten what that man had done to him or how it made him feel. I've often wondered if that's why Dad didn't become a Christian until he was in his 40's. Thankfully, there were many other old men in that community who loved Dad and took a special interest in helping Grandmother raise him. Dad spoke of these men who were good to him with great fondness his entire life. Kids never forget the people who are good to them, and they never forget the people who mistreat them.

> *"And whosoever shall offend one of these little*
> *ones that believe in me, it is better for him that*
> *a millstone were hanged about his neck, and*
> *he were cast into the sea" (Mark 9:42).*

14

Leave Earlier

"If you're in a hurry – leave earlier."
Papaw

Papaw would not be late. He started to work at Pet Milk Incorporated when he was sixteen and retired from there when he was sixty-five. He left for work every morning long before it was necessary to get to work on time. He believed you should leave early enough for any destination that you would have time to stop and change a flat tire and still be on time.

He drove slower than most people. Any discussion about his pace would be met with these words, *"If you're in a hurry – leave earlier."* That was an entrenched philosophy of life with him. He always stayed busy, but he was seldom in a rush. If you were not fifteen minutes early to any appointment, to the old man, you were late.

If you want to know how important pacing yourself in life is, look up the statistics on how many vehicle-related deaths are due to excessive speed. When you rush through life, you make mistakes. This applies to travel as well as decision-making on important matters. Planning ahead, getting up early, and taking your time are literally life-saving and stress-reducing formulas for living. The old man never took one of those time management classes, but he was wise enough to figure it out for himself. Like the old man, I hate leaving late. I hate rushing. I hate being late for anything. Being late is poor character and rudeness to those waiting on you.

"So teach us to number our days, that we may apply our hearts unto wisdom" (Psalm 90:12).

15

Change Your Oil

"Changing the oil is the life of a vehicle."
Dad

Dad almost always bought new vehicles. He worked extremely hard, sometimes holding three jobs – law enforcement, as well as taxidermy and farming, which were seasonal. He didn't like to buy used cars, because he thought you were just buying other people's junk. No matter how long he kept a vehicle, he kept it in immaculate condition.

His vehicles were kept clean inside and out. He had a 1974 Bronco that he used to hunt in the mountains. Under the seat of that Bronco was a meat cleaver wrapped in an old white T-shirt. When he got on a brushy road with his Bronco, he would use that meat cleaver to trim back the brush to keep from scratching his hunting vehicle. The reason he owned the Bronco was so that he wouldn't have to drive his truck in the mountains. That's still funny to me, but that was Terry Jones.

He often said, *"Changing the oil is the life of a vehicle."* He was fanatical about it and changed his own oil until he got up in years and was too sick. Every three thousand miles, he changed his oil like clockwork. He kept them vacuumed and washed externally. In the door of his truck, which I drive now, there is a medicine bottle where he saved quarters so that he could regularly stop at car washes and take care of business. If the state of Tennessee salted the roads in bad weather, he would carefully wash the undercarriage of the vehicle to prevent rust.

He bought a used Bronco in the mid 80's to replace another that he had sold. He took that used Bronco apart piece by piece down to the chassis in his driveway. He then sand-blasted all the rust off and coated everything with undercoating of some sort. By the time he was finished, the Bronco looked brand new, and he placed his meat cleaver under the seat.

The old men grew up poor, and they knew they had to make stuff last. Even when they got to the place in life that they could afford new vehicles, they still maintained them like they had to last them the rest of their lives. When Dad traded in an old vehicle on a new one, the dealership was always thrilled to get it. Life requires maintenance too. Keeping things that are harmful to us cleaned out and renewing our minds with the Word of God daily keeps life running on all eight cylinders. Maintenance allows for peak performance.

"For which cause we faint not; but though our outward man perish, yet the inward man is renewed day by day" (2 Corinthians 4:16).

16

Move Real Slow

"Move real slow."
Dad

Dad taught me deer hunting in the rugged mountains, not down on the farmland where deer are easier prey. The deer Dad hunted were extremely adept at staying alive. They were what folks around here call "spooky". The slightest hint of human presence, and they could be gone in a flash.

Dad's hunting method was simple. He would find a place in the mountains with some deer sign. Then he'd look for a "low gap" between two higher peaks that would allow deer an easier route across the mountain. Way before daylight, he'd set up an ambush point among the thick laurel bushes and set up for the day. He'd gently push all the fallen leaves and sticks back in an area big enough for us both and then spread an old military tarp out for us to sit on. He taught me that any movement I made for the entire day must be made very slowly. I mean *extremely* slow. We would sit on that tarp quietly until darkness covered us again.

Dad's deer hunting methodology was deadly. He killed deer on a regular basis even when populations were low. His secret was patience. He would sit in those low gaps day after day knowing at some point the deer would pass through. Dad served his country in the jungles of Vietnam, and I've wondered if he learned to survive by not being seen.

Life requires patience. Rash people make a lot of mistakes that patient people don't. How many people crash cars simply because they pass another vehicle when they shouldn't. Slow down. Think things through. Move slowly. Wait on the Lord.

"Be patient therefore, brethren, unto the coming of the Lord. Behold, the husbandman waiteth for the precious fruit of the earth, and hath long patience for it, until he receive the early and latter rain" (James 5:7).

17

Know God

*"Get to know God, and you'll know
God's will for your life."*
Dr. Darrell Champlin (Missionary)

One of the greatest privileges I've had in life is knowing men who love the Lord and give their lives to serve Him. Among those great servants of the Lord that I had the opportunity to spend time with was a missionary name Dr. Darrell Champlin. This book could not contain the incredible stories associated with Dr. Champlin and the mission work he did in Africa and South America. His spiritual battles with witch doctors in the jungles are legendary.

God had already called me to the ministry, and I was in college studying for the task at hand when I first met Dr. Champlin. Listening to his experiences in some of the remote places on earth blew my mind. Eventually, I would spend five weeks with his family in the cities and jungles of Suriname, South America, and all that I'd heard would come to life.

For some time, I had been trying to decide my next move after college. I figured a man like Dr. Champlin would be a good man from which to get counsel, so I approached him with a simple question. I asked him, "How can I know God's will for my life?" I'm not sure what I expected him to say. Possibly, I was hoping for some kind of practical formula that I could apply. Instead, he gave a one sentence answer that I was not expecting, *"Get to know God, and you'll know God's will for your life."* The old missionary man was right. I didn't need a formula; I needed a better relationship with my God. I needed to know Him well enough to hear His voice and follow it. Knowing God is the greatest pursuit of life.

"And ye shall seek me, and find me, when ye shall search for me with all your heart" (Jeremiah 29:13).

18

Common Sense

"Some people are educated beyond their intelligence."
Dr. David Baughan (Evangelist)

The old men I grew up with didn't lay claim to having much formal education. Their book learning, as they called it, mostly ranged from near zero to my dad eventually earning an associate degree in criminal justice. Later in life, I spent several years in college surrounded by people with degrees, including many with earned doctorates.

I found out that the old men I grew up with were just as wise as those with a formal education. In fact, some of those with a degree in the secular colleges I attended were willfully ignorant. They were detrimental to themselves and the students they attempted to teach.

One professor I had named Dr. David Baughan was from Pratt, WV. He was a rare combination of man filled both with common sense and book learning. Concerning those who had a formal education but were devoid of common sense, he would say, *"Some people are educated beyond their intelligence."* These are the kind of people with medical degrees who seemingly don't know the biological differences between genders. I've never met a "hillbilly" family that didn't know the gender of their children. Who's more intelligent? Frankly, a lot of young people are being destroyed by foolish people posing as experts on America's college campuses.

Don't be impressed with degrees. Don't be impressed with titles. Don't be impressed with positions. If you're going to allow an old man to influence you, make sure it's one with good common sense. If he happens to have a formal education to go along with that common sense, that's just fine.

"Professing themselves to be wise, they became fools" (Romans 1:22).

19

Look For Yourself

"Let's see what they are running."
Dad

Experts are considered experts for a reason, but even the experts can be wrong. It's important in life that you learn to learn from experts but also learn not to lean on them, without regard to your own good judgment. An unwillingness to listen to old men, who are the very best in their field, will cost you countless wasted years; you will learn things from scratch that others could have taught you in twenty minutes. Just make sure you don't give them such a place of prominence in your life that they can't be questioned.

Dad wasn't one to be late for anything important, but one day we got to the mountain well after daylight. A bear track had been found, and dogs were already in pursuit. As we approached the area where the race was taking place, we heard an old bear hunter, a true expert, warn everyone that the dogs had messed up and were not running a bear. He said they were running a deer. Running anything but a bear for a bear dog is bad medicine. If I had been alone that day, I would've simply taken the old bear hunters' word for it and ignored that pack of dogs.

Dad, being somewhat of an expert himself, didn't think the other bear hunter was right. He said, *"Let's see what they are running."* Within just a few minutes, Dad had positioned us right below the dogs, and, in a wink, Old Slew Foot came into sight. Right in front of those dogs was a bear – not a deer. As good as the old bear hunter was, he had misjudged the situation and just about let a bear get away. Instead, Dad followed his own instincts, and a dead bear lay at our feet.

Sometimes two old men who are both genuine experts on a matter will see things differently. Neither of them is always right all the time. Listen to the experts. Respect the experts. Yet never surrender your obligation to question matters of life and check things out for yourself.

> *"Search the scriptures; for in them ye think ye have eternal life: and they are they which testify of me" (John 5:39).*

20

That's All We Have

"That will have to work – it's all we have."
Papaw

Papaw was born in 1928 in an economically poor area of East Tennessee. He was literally born in the mountains on a small farm. Resources were scarce. The mountain people had to do the best they could with whatever they could afford. My family wouldn't have taken welfare even if it had been available.

I can't remember the exact details of the conversation now, but it had something to do with a farm project we were attempting to accomplish. Papaw was doing the project in some way that seemed unnecessarily difficult to me because of the resources we were using. I suggested that we make a run to town and buy better materials to make the job easier. Of course, that was easy for me to say because I wasn't the one having to foot the bill.

Papaw made it clear that we would use what we had. I decided to make my case again by saying, "That won't work." By this time, the old man was irritated with my position and vehemently stated, *"It has to work – that's all we've got."* His world and my world had collided. In his world of the Great Depression, you didn't just run to town and get stuff to make life easier. In my world things had been a little easier and certainly more abundant. Papaw was a very patient and gentle man, so when he did get mad, you knew to pull up and pay attention.

Papaw absolutely was going to get the job done with the resources already available. And he did. Often in life, to be successful, it's not a thing that we need, it's a stronger will and a better work ethic.

"Be ye strong therefore, and let not your hands be weak: for your work shall be rewarded" (II Chronicles 15:7).

21

Money and Decisions

*"Never make a major decision based
primarily on finances."*
Dr. Ron Comfort (Evangelist)

Dr. Comfort was the president of the college I attended. On several occasions I heard him say, *"Never make a major decision based primarily on finances."* There is a reason the Bible says, "the love of money is the root of all evil."

Money itself isn't evil. Having money isn't evil. Many of the godliest people in the Bible were extremely wealthy. Loving money is what's evil. Once a person falls in love with money, they are controlled by it. The endless pursuit of getting more money and holding on to that money has destroyed countless lives. Money is necessary to some extent, but it's also very limited in its abilities. It can buy your bread, but it can't satisfy you with the bread. It can allow you to have a variety of experiences, but it can't make you enjoy those experiences. It can even attract the opposite sex into a relationship, but it can't put love into that relationship.

Major decisions should be based on one thing for a Christian – God's will. If something is God's will, He will supply everything necessary to accomplish that will. Dr. Comfort's advice about money and decisions has been a guiding principle for me. I've never been financially wealthy, but I've been able to live with peace in my heart knowing I sought to follow God and knowing He promised to meet my needs.

"For the love of money is the root of all evil: which while some coveted after, they have erred from the faith, and pierced themselves through with many sorrows" (I Timothy 6:10).

Evangelist Ron Comfort

22

My Allowance

*"Your allowance is the food on the table
and the roof over your head."*
Dad

Dad and I had finished working on the farm and were in his truck, just pulling onto the road to head home, when I decided to ask for a regular allowance. I'm not sure where I got the idea about allowances, and I'm not certain why I chose that day to ask. Maybe I thought I'd earned some remuneration based on the farm work that day.

Dad's answer was short and to the point, *"Your allowance is the food on the table and the roof over your head."* I made no attempt to negotiate. Dad's demeanor made it clear that his answer was final. Truthfully, I understood. We weren't a rich family. Dad worked almost every waking hour to provide for us in multiple ways. Mom always had a full-time job too. My parents were good providers. We had a nice home, good clothes and plenty to eat. And we had things beyond our needs. All those provisions came through work. My parents didn't owe me anything, and I knew it.

*"And having food and raiment let us be
therewith content" (I Timothy 6:8).*

23

Early to Bed

"Nothing good happens after dark."
Papaw

U nless he was doing some type of law enforcement work which kept him out late, Papaw would always be in bed by 8-8:30PM. He firmly believed that laying out at night was detrimental to people. He would say, *"Nothing good happens after dark."* The old man was on to something there.

One year around the Christmas season, Papaw and I had plans to bear hunt on a particular Saturday. Papaw informed me he wouldn't be able to go, which was highly unusual. He explained that my younger cousin, also his grandson, would be in from South Carolina, and he needed to spend the day with him.

Saturday morning Papaw walked through the front door but didn't have my cousin with him. He said my cousin had laid out all night and was still in bed. Honestly, I was a little aggravated by that. I didn't like canceling our hunt only to miss it because my cousin wanted to ramble all night. Later that day I asked my cousin what time he got home. He got home at 8:30PM, but Papaw was already in bed. It was hilarious to us, but we both respected the ways of the old man.

That may seem a little strange to some folks, but it is really good advice from the old man. Getting home and getting to bed is a much better philosophy than running the roads in the late hours of the night, drinking or doing some other foolishness that leads to no good. Maybe that's old-fashioned thinking, but it's really practical.

> *"In the twilight, in the evening, in the black and dark night" (Proverbs 7:9).*

24

Find the Elk First

"Find the elk before you leave the truck."
Philip Syck

I have a brother-in-law who is an extremely effective elk hunter. His percentage of success is insane, compared to Montana state averages of other hunters. When I moved to Montana, I spent as much time with him as possible in reference to elk hunting. When I start to learn something new, I try to learn from the best person I can get advice from, no matter what the subject happens to be.

Elk and deer were important to my family during our time in Montana. My wife and I had 3 children on a relatively low income, and groceries were not cheap. We ate a lot of wild game. Deer were amazingly abundant and easy to kill. Elk were fairly abundant but not so easy to kill. The most important tip I was given was when Philip said this, *"Find the elk before you leave the truck."*

Some of the best elk hunters in my area spent countless hours glassing the mountains for elk from the road. Once they located a herd, they would watch them day after day in the pre-season, until they patterned the daily movements of those elk. Once season opened, they put their boots on the ground to get in position to kill an elk, instead of wasting time meandering through the mountains hoping to stumble upon a herd.

There are other successful methods of elk hunting. Those methods are also best learned by following the skillful example and advice of someone who is actually successful. This is the same for just about every area in life. I'm amazed at how many people either choose to learn the hard way or take advice from those who know absolutely nothing about the subject they think they have mastered! If you want to kill elk, learn from someone who kills elk. If you want a successful marriage, learn from someone who's had a successful marriage. If you want to live for Christ, seek the company of those who walk with Christ.

*"Be ye followers of me, even as I also
am of Christ" (I Corinthians 11:1).*

Philip Syck - the best elk hunter I know.

25

Doing Things Right the First Time

"If you're going to do something, do it right the first time, and you won't have to do it again."

Dad

Of all the things Dad said to me, the quote above is the one I think of most often. It was one of the driving principles of his life. I never heard my dad use the word excellence, but he was a man who practiced excellence in everything he approached in life. If he did anything, he was going to do the best he could, and he hated having to redo things.

When Dad got dressed, it could take him up to an hour to shower, shave, trim his mustache and comb his hair. Everything about his appearance was important to him. He kept his pocket knife sharp. His vehicles were clean inside and out. If he was doing mundane farm work, it would be done right with no shortcuts. He taught himself to do taxidermy work and became so good at it that locals began bringing him their game animals to mount. Doing things right was his way.

This philosophy of doing things right rings through my head nearly every day of my life. I'm not claiming I've lived up to Dad's high-water mark of excellence, but I can say, I never escape his voice telling me to do it right no matter the task.

"Whatsoever thy hand findeth to do, do it with thy might; for there is no work, nor device, nor knowledge, nor wisdom, in the grave, whither thou goest" (Ecclesiastes 9:10).

26

Going to Church

*"Going to church is like going to Sunday dinner.
If you go, you get fed. If you don't, you go hungry."*
Papaw

Papaw was a faithful church going man. It was rare for him to miss a service. He went Sunday morning, Sunday evening and Wednesday night, like clockwork. Church, to Papaw, wasn't a matter of convenience; it was a matter of necessity. He believed that faithfully attending church and hearing the Bible preach fed a man's soul, and without it, he hungered spiritually.

Most of my weekends were spent at my grandparents' home. Papaw would pick me up Friday evening after school and I'd stay until Sunday afternoon. He required me to go to church with him. I didn't like church. There was no particular reason I didn't like church; it just didn't interest me. Some of the best people in our community attended that church. Several of them would eventually become some of the most meaningful people in my life. Papaw would bribe me into going to church by letting me drive there in his truck. People would go nuts today if a ten-year-old boy pulled in driving a Ford F-150, but times were different then.

One summer during Vacation Bible School that church gave me a Frisbee that had John 3:16 written on it. I played catch with that yellow frisbee with a Boston Terrier dog I had. I read John 3:16 over and over. I didn't know much about God, but I knew that verse said he loved people. Looking back, I believe God used that church and that Bible verse on the frisbee to plant a seed in my heart that would eventually bring me to salvation in Christ. John 3:16 is still my favorite verse.

Amazingly, after I trusted Christ as my Savior, I fell in love with church! I loved the people. All of a sudden, I enjoyed preaching. I had a million questions for the Pastor. I'd go early and sit outside just to be there. The church is the bride of Christ. When you fall in love with Christ, you'll also fall in love with his bride.

Lots of people today see little value in attending church. They're wrong, *plain wrong!* Every Christian needs to be in church on a regular basis. It should be a priority. Parents are failing their children if they don't have them in a good Bible preaching church. Dads should lead the way. Church isn't just for women and children. Church is for real men too. The man who lives his life apart from church will live spiritually anemic. I'm thankful for the example the old man set every Sunday morning when he pointed his truck toward that little mountain church. I'm even more thankful he required me to be in the passenger seat with him.

"Not forsaking the assembling of ourselves together, as the manner of some is; but exhorting one another: and so much the more, as ye see the day approaching" (Hebrews 10:25).

27

Playing Hurt

"You're a pansy."
Dad

During a little league baseball game, I was behind the plate catching. There was a runner on third, and our team really needed to keep him from scoring. At the crack of the bat the runner on third headed for home, full steam. One of our fielders made a play and rifled the ball to me. It was going to be close, so I had the plate completely blocked with ball in glove. The runner's legs somehow twisted around my left arm and snapped it. I didn't know it was broken, but I knew it hurt.

The game still had innings to go, and I stayed in the game. When the ball hit my glove, I couldn't squeeze it tight enough to catch it, so the ball just stopped with a thud and dropped to the ground. I finished the game with a broke catching arm, and thankfully, we won the game. My team, the Camp Creek Bears, were not normally the best team in the league, but that year we won the regular season championship.

After the game, my dad and I arrived home at the same time. As I opened the door, he was standing right behind me. Opening that door sent a sharp pain up my broken arm, and I verbalized my pain. Dad asked what was wrong, and I told him I hurt my arm playing baseball. His response was typical for the old men I now hold in high regard. He said, *"You're a pansy."* A lot of people who read this will think that this was cruel. That's because they don't understand the importance of old men helping boys toughen up for life. Boys can't be sissies if they are going to become men. Neither of us knew my arm was broken. Dad just thought I was being a whiner, and he wasn't having it.

The next day I went fishing at a place called Luke's Mill. Davy Crockett's family had owned a mill there many years before Luke Fillers operated his mill. Just above the mill was a pond with good fishing. I caught a bass, and when I set the hook, the pain hit me again. I stopped reeling my line and ran up through the field with my pole until I landed the fish. It was a couple mile walk home, and as soon as I got there, I called Mom, who was at work. She made arrangements for me to go to the Emergency Room where they X-rayed my arm, verified it was broken, and put a cast on it. When I saw Dad that afternoon, I held up my cast and said to him, "There's your pansy."

Dad didn't consider my response as being disrespectful. He was a full-grown man. He knew he had wrongly accused me of being a sissy when the opposite was actually true. I had earned the right to speak up for myself. These are the times when old men are the proudest of their boys even if they don't say it. Some women and weak men can have a hard time understanding this dynamic. Boys must grow up and live and work in the real world. Life isn't easy. Boys need to get tough enough to play hurt. The old men know it.

"Watch ye, stand fast in the faith, quit you like men, be strong" (I Corinthians 16:13).

28

Frugalness

"It's not what you make that matters; it's what you save."
Papaw

I don't pretend to be a financial wizard. I'm in no position to give advice on getting rich or being a successful investor. When it comes to money, the Lord has always provided for me as I needed it. My Papaw had a lot to say about money, and much of what he said makes more sense to me now that I'm older than when I was younger.

One thing he said that I think deserves attention is this: *"It's not what you make that matters; it's what you save."* Remember my Papaw was born into a poverty-stricken Appalachian family in 1928. The Great Depression was 1929-1939. His introduction to life was to a world with sparse resources and few opportunities.

He took his first public job at Pet Milk Incorporated when he was 16. The minimum wage in 1944 was $0.30 per hour. Papaw survived and I would say thrived based on two financial principles – 1. Hard work 2. Frugalness. He built his family home, provided basic needs, kept decent vehicles, took family vacations and bought a sixty-seven-acre farm making low wages. His two daughters would tell you he took very good care of them even beyond meeting their needs.

He said that if you were given a raise at work, you should save the amount of the raise and continue to live off your original salary. He did well at his job and would retire, not as a low- wage employee, but as a laboratory technician with a solid pay rate. Although he only had a grade school education, his position in the lab required new employees to have a college degree.

Hard work and frugalness are great companions. That formula has been a success story for many Americans coming out of The Great Depression. If you're just getting started in life, and you're wondering how to make it in economically hard times, this is a good place to start. You can add other economic skills to this well-founded basis later as you go. The old man built a great life for his family out of nearly nothing.

"Go to the ant, thou sluggard; consider
her way, and be wise:
Which having no guide, overseer, or ruler,
provideth her meat in the summer, and gathereth
her food in the harvest" (Proverbs 6:6-8).

29

The Birds and the Bees

"I'm glad you like girls."
Dr. John Godfrey

Pastor John Godfrey was my senior pastor in Chesapeake, VA. He is a wealth of knowledge on the home, husband-wife relationships, and raising children. He's recognized by his peers as being practically helpful on these topics and is often invited to be a guest speaker by other pastors to address them.

During one of our many discussions, we had a conversation about the trouble boys are having today with pornography. As the discussion broadened, Pastor Godfrey made this statement, tongue in cheek, *"It used to be if you caught a boy with pornography, you were really upset. Now the first thing you want to tell that boy is that you're glad he likes girls."* That was a sobering moment for me. Of course, Godfrey was using some sarcasm to illustrate how things had so drastically changed morally. He wasn't suggesting that we make light of pornography. He was stating the obvious in an unforgettable way – bad has gone to worse.

The seeds of the 1960's sexual revolution were now bearing fruit – rotten fruit. Sexual deviancy of every sort is now crammed down the throats of children at such an early age, they're robbed of their innocence before they can turn five. Children should be allowed to be children, not targeted by all sorts of perverts and perversions. Let them grow up. Let them become adults. Our society needs to put a full stop to the exploitation of children by people whose lives are defined by sexual deviance. It's my opinion that any adult convicted of child molestation should face the death penalty by the legal authorities.

The "birds and the bees" need to be discussed, but that's the responsibility of parents at the appropriate age. Christian parents in particular want to see their children taught God's perspective on sex, gender and marital relationships. Pastor Godfrey challenged young men to view sex as good in the context of marriage and admonished them to wait on reality instead of sinfully participating in fantasy. Old Men ought to take on the responsibility of protecting their boys and girls from anyone who would exploit them with wicked views in these areas. God help us.

"So God created man in his own image, in the image of God created he him; male and female created he them"
(Genesis 1:27).

30

Don't Quit

"You're not coming home."
Dr. Jerry Mullendore

T he Bible college I attended was very strict. Prior to going to college, I was working a full-time job there and attending East Tennessee State University. I was living for the Lord and preaching in country churches all over our area. I didn't go to Bible college because I needed a babysitter. I went there to learn the Word of God, so I would be better prepared to fulfill the calling He had placed on my life. At the beginning of my first semester, I was absolutely floored by all the rules they had for every aspect of life, and I didn't quite understand some of the applications they made of certain portions of Scripture.

I had more freedoms as a 10-year-old in some ways than full-grown men had in that college. It was a lot for me to internalize in such a short time. I grew frustrated and angry over what I considered unnecessary control. I decided that I had made a mistake in attending that particular college and determined to leave. I called my Pastor, Jerry Mullendore, and told him I was moving back to Tennessee.

His response was not what I expected. He rebuked me strongly, and in no uncertain terms told me, *"You're not coming home."* We politely debated the matter over the phone. He wouldn't relent his position. He understood the transitions that I was going through. His experience in ministry and manhood knew that I needed what I was going to learn and experience at that college, and if he could stop me from quitting, he was going to do it. Out of respect for his opinion, I decided to stay. I'm glad I did.

Over the course of my studies, I learned there were very serious reasons while the college was so strict. I also learned that some of the applications they made of Scripture were good, solid applications, and I had lacked the discernment to know it. I'm not saying I adopted every detail of the college's philosophy of ministry, but the time I spent there helped me immensely. I didn't know it when I enrolled, but that college was basically the Marine Boot Camp of Baptist Colleges. They were not playing games. They intended on equipping men for ministry and developing men who could handle the spiritual battle ahead.

Frank Camp, Mike Westmorland, Jerry Mullendore and TL Jones. Mike and TL were ordained to the gospel ministry on this day.

Quitting when things get hard is not an option for a pastor. Ministry is a fight with all the forces of Hell. Christians are in a war over the souls of men. Satan will test the mettle of everyone who seeks to serve the Lord. If I had quit college, I likely would've eventually quit the ministry too. The old man put his foot down with me. He rebuked me. This was done in love. He didn't want me to be a quitter. I thank God that old man stepped into my life at a weak moment and barked some backbone into my life.

"If thou hast run with the footmen, and they have wearied thee, then how canst thou contend with horses? and if in the land of peace, wherein thou trustedst, they wearied thee, then how wilt thou do in the swelling of Jordan?" (Jeremiah 12:5)

31

Laziness

"Did you ride that three-wheeler to the mailbox?"
Dad

In 1985, I came home from high school to an awesome surprise. My parents had bought a brand-new Honda Big Red three-wheeler. I was stoked. That thing was so much fun!

That winter we got a good snow. East Tennessee doesn't get snow like Wisconsin does, but every so often we get a good 8-10 inches. When that happens people of all ages find some way to play in it. The Honda Big Red was awesome in the snow.

One afternoon I was told to go to the mailbox and bring in the day's mail. The mailbox was only fifty yards or so from the house, but I couldn't resist jumping on the Big Red and playing for a bit while I was outside. I didn't ride it because I was too lazy to walk to the mailbox. It was just fun waiting to happen, and I thought nothing of firing it up and playing a while.

When I came inside with the mail, Dad was waiting for me. He was unamused. He asked me, *"Did you ride that three-wheeler to the mailbox?"* I obviously had. He knew I had. The question was rhetorical. In Dad's mind, he assumed that his son was so lazy that he wouldn't even walk fifty yards to the mailbox. He was wrong, but that didn't stop him from grounding me from using the three-wheeler for some time. I think I got grounded for a full month.

Though that was an unjust deal based on a wrong assumption, it did reinforce an unfaltering principle that dad lived by – *laziness was not acceptable.* Even the possibility of laziness was going to be addressed. He worked. Mom worked. I wasn't going to be a slacker under his watch. I'm sure I was mad about the ordeal at the time, but whatever frustration I may have had then has turned to appreciation over time. The old man despised laziness. I got it.

"He also that is slothful in his work is brother to him that is a great waster" (Proverbs 18:9).

32

Awareness

"If you're standing in a group of men and one of them keeps his hands in his pockets, keep your eye on him."
Papaw

The Appalachians were not always the fun of Gatlinburg or the serenity of the well-paved Blue Ridge Parkway. There have been dark and murderous times in these mountains. During my Papaw's formative years, the illegal moonshine trade created a lot of sorrow, death and destruction. As he would say, "There were a lot of killings." Even today, I could take you to many locations where people were murdered. Papaw was a man of keen awareness. As a constable, law enforcement officer, he experienced his share of dangerous encounters. He was a survivor, and he wanted me to know how to keep myself out of harm's way.

He once said to me, *"If you're standing in a group of men and one of them keeps his hands in his pockets, keep your eye on him."* The man with his hands in his pockets possibly had a snub nose .38 or a hawk bill knife. If you watched him, and he drew his weapon, you'd be able to respond quickly enough to potentially save your life, while everyone else was caught off guard. Nearly 40 years have passed since Papaw told me that, and I still keep a close eye on anyone I'm around. Because Papaw and Dad were both law enforcement, I often wondered if I'd run into someone who wanted to get revenge on them by taking it on me. As a teenager when I walked the Appalachian Trail hunting, I'd always have my rifle ready. Even now I think ahead about my surroundings and pay careful attention to potential threats. *I'm not afraid, but I am aware,* and where I view a potential threat from an individual, I'm always thinking of a way to eliminate the threat if needed.

American children are growing up in dangerous times. The drug cartels have made most every place in America somewhat dangerous. You simply never know who you'll run up against. Our children can't be raised like sheep and sent out to the wolves. They need reality explained to them and taught to keep themselves aware of their surroundings. People are continuously being robbed, raped and murdered because they don't have the sense to survey a situation and handle it appropriately.

Spiritually speaking we're also the target of Satan. He hunts like a lion after prey. Being aware of this danger and preparing ourselves with the whole armor of God is our defense. Physically and spiritually awareness is a life saver.

*"Be sober, be vigilant; because your adversary
the devil, as a roaring lion, walketh about,
seeking whom he may devour" (I Peter 5:8).*

33

No Windows

*"Something just wasn't right. They didn't
have any windows in the building."*
Dad

Dad began his law enforcement career as a jailer. He eventually worked his way up through the ranks, becoming the chief jailer. Later, he switched from the jail to being a patrolman, and again, advanced upward, becoming a Sergeant and then a Lieutenant. He would eventually run for office and win the election to become Sheriff. During his election campaign, he was invited by a group of men to attend some type of religious organization.

When he received the invitation, I was away at college, but we discussed the invitation by phone. At the time, Dad wasn't a Christian, and I was concerned he'd get sucked into some type of false religion. He decided to accept the invitation despite my dissenting opinion.

After he attended the event, we discussed the matter again. I asked him what he thought about the sect. I was delightfully surprised by his discernment. He said, *"Something wasn't right.*

They didn't have any windows in the building." **Although Dad** wasn't a deeply spiritual man and had little Bible knowledge, his steadfast common sense had won the day for him. He reasoned that any group of people who had to practice their beliefs in secret were up to no good. Dad didn't know it at the time, but he had hit on one of the great truths about the character and nature of the living God. God is light, and in him is no darkness at all! God's people are not instructed to hide from the world. They're instructed to be the light of the world! The old man may not have been a trained theologian, but his common sense was keen.

"This then is the message which we have heard of him, and declare unto you, that God is light, and in him is no darkness at all" (I John 1:5).

34

Laughter is Like Medicine

*"All I know is that fifteen minutes of my life
is gone, and I don't remember a thing."*
Steve Bowman

O ur next-door neighbor was a United States Forest Officer named Steve Bowman. Steve was a fantastic neighbor and a close personal friend with Dad. As a law enforcement officer, Steve wasn't always liked by others in our community, but I knew him outside of his official capacity. He was one of the funniest people I've ever known.

I would purposely watch for him to come home from work and try to catch him before he could make it into his basement. I'm sure there were times where he'd see me coming and dread getting caught again. His stories made me laugh so hard my side would hurt. Anytime I could grab a few minutes to listen to him, I wasn't going to miss it.

He told me a story about another kid shooting his eyeglasses out in a school gymnasium during a basketball game that was crazy. Another favorite was his dad smoking hams in an old panel truck all winter and the dogs chasing his dad down the road in the spring due to the smell of the truck. One of the funniest stories was about a time he went to a hypnotist hoping the hypnosis would help him quit smoking. It's an absolutely hilarious story that ended with Steve saying, *"All I know is that fifteen minutes of my life is gone, and I don't remember a thing."*

Laughter is an essential part of life. I personally believe that human laughter is proof of the existence of God. Steve was one of the old men in my life that made life better just by laughing. I'm sure his stories were greatly exaggerated just for the sake of entertainment, and I loved him for it.

Steve was tragically killed in a helicopter crash in East Tennessee. He was part of an operation searching for illegal marijuana patches on forest reserve property. Evidently, the helicopter had a mechanical malfunction, and Steve and the pilot were killed in the line of duty. I accompanied my dad next door to tell Steve's family he was missing in a crash and a search was under way. The panic on his young son's face has haunted me since. It took a few days to find the missing helicopter in the thick rugged mountains, and Dad and I assisted the search parties in looking for Steve and his pilot. I later received a letter of gratitude from the United States National Forest for my efforts in the search. At Steve's funeral, a man played Amazing Grace on the bagpipes, and I wept bitter tears.

Steve's wild stories were a big part of my life as a teenager. You can be a serious man with a serious job but still be able to laugh. Laughter is more important than we give it credit. I knew other old men with a healthy sense of humor. They added value to my life.

"A merry heart doeth good like a medicine: but a broken spirit drieth the bones" (Proverbs 17:22).

35

Grace

"Is that all there is to it?"
T.W. Brown

Uncle T.W. Brown was my aunt's husband on my momma's side. He grew up near a small town called Bethune, SC. I don't know a lot about his upbringing, but from what I do know, it was pretty rough. Uncle T.W. spent more than a few years of his life on the wild side of things. Somewhere along the way he had gotten so low that he had the words "Born to Die" tattooed on his arm.

When I was in college, I got a phone call from the family telling me Uncle T.W. was in the hospital and not doing well. I can't remember the circumstances of his hospitalization. The Lord led me to make the drive to South Carolina to visit with him for the express purpose of talking to him about his soul.

Uncle T.W., although rough around the edges, had a fear of God and respect for me as a preacher. When I arrived at the hospital, he was completely open to me taking a Bible and showing him how to be saved. During the discussion he had a question about the Old Testament law. He was somewhat confused about the difference between works and grace. This type of confusion is very common. Uncle T.W. thought there must be something he needed to "do" to earn salvation. I took the time to share some verses with him from Galatians, explaining to him that the Old Testament law was a schoolmaster to bring us to Christ, not a means of salvation.

Grace is undeserved favor. Grace cannot be earned. Grace cannot be bought. Grace is when God gives you something you don't deserve. No human being deserves salvation, because we are all sinners. We deserve eternal punishment in Hell because of our sin. But Jesus came and died for our sin. He took our punishment for us when He was crucified. His blood was payment for our sins. God can give us salvation by grace because Jesus paid for it.

TW Brown

I can still remember seeing the light come on in Uncle T.W.'s eyes. In a very exact instant, the Holy Spirit helped him understand the concept of salvation by grace, and he received Christ as his Savior at that moment. His words to me were, *"Is that all there is to it?"* I assured him that grace was the offer, and it was received by faith. Uncle T.W. was a different man after that. He eventually became a member of a Baptist church and served the Lord by watching after the church's graveyard. When he passed away years later, I was privileged to preach his funeral. Uncle T.W. didn't know it in his rowdy years, but he wasn't "Born to Die" as his tattoo said. He was born again to live! Grace made the difference for him. Grace can make the difference for you too.

"For by grace are ye saved through faith; and that not of yourselves: it is the gift of God: Not of works, lest any man should boast" (Ephesians 2:8-9).

36

Wicked Women

*"The devil doesn't always wear overalls.
Sometimes he wears a dress."*
Pastor Marvin Whitt

Pastor Whitt was my second pastor. The old man who led me to Christ had a stroke and died, and Pastor Whitt was elected soon after. Pastor Whitt was a man of strong Bible conviction, sound wisdom and a fantastic sense of humor. He spent a lot of time mentoring me in my early days as a Christian.

One of his sayings that stuck with me was this, *"The devil doesn't always wear overalls. Sometimes he wears a dress."* Pastor Whitt wasn't a male chauvinist, and he wasn't one who belittled women. He just understood that not all women are the same. In my opinion, a godly woman is the apex of God's creation. Nothing on earth compares to a good woman, and in constraint to that, a wicked woman is the downfall of many a poor boy. When King Solomon wrote Proverbs to help his own son navigate the pitfalls of life, he warned much about strange women.

Old men need to talk to boys about these kinds of real-life scenarios the same way Solomon sought to speak to his son.

Every generation has gullible boys and strange women. Boys need it explained in clear terms what's what. This subject has no place for being vague or politically correct. Some women are evil. Some of them are predatory in nature and seek out gullible young men for devious purposes. Even a mighty man like Samson was no match for cunning Delilah.

Pastor Whitt's old fashioned country wisdom was dead on. Over the years I've seen countless situations unfold, where it was obvious the powers of darkness were using a woman to accomplish ungodly things. It's a tale as old as time. Satan keeps using the same tactic, because it's so effective.

"That they may keep thee from the strange woman, from the stranger which flattereth with her words" (Proverbs 7:7).

37

Personal Accountability

"If you get cancer, don't come crying to me."
Dad

I was somewhere around the fifth grade the first time I chewed tobacco. After school, I went home with a friend one afternoon to just loaf around. We ended up tramping around in the woods with an old .22 rifle, seeing what we could find to shoot. If that seems too young to be in the woods with a rifle, that's only because, as we say in the mountains, "You ain't from around here".

In addition to the rifle, my buddy also brought along some chewing tobacco. Although my family grew tobacco as a cash crop, I was highly discouraged from using it. On this day, I decided I'd dismiss all the warnings I'd been given and try it for myself. Unfortunately, I liked it.

When I got to my teen years, I became a regular user of tobacco but hid it from my parents. They had caught me on multiple occasions, but nothing they said or did deterred me from it. I wasn't characteristically a rebel against my parents. They were good parents, and I loved and respected them both, but the tobacco issue was simple – I liked chewing it.

The last time Mom found my hidden tobacco she turned the matter over to Dad. He called me into the living room and expressed his disappointment in my behavior. However, this time there wasn't going to be another lecture. This is where the lectures stopped. I was around sixteen and Dad decided enough was enough with the tobacco hide and seek game. He said to me, very somberly, *"If you get cancer, don't come crying to me."* And that was the end of it. Neither parent ever brought it up again, and from that time forward, I chewed openly. Dad had decided to take the pressure off himself and mom and put the pressure on me. He was telling me that it was time to take responsibility for my own actions, and that he was going to let me.

From that day forward, I chewed as I wanted, and when I did, I thought of Dad's words. When I was hiding from them, I was just trying to do as I wished. But now that there was no penalty for chewing, I began to be conscious of the penalty of my choices. Every time I had a dry mouth, I'd think it may be cancer. When my throat was sore, I thought I may have cancer. And If I did get cancer, it would be entirely my fault, and Dad didn't want to hear any whining about it. Dad had made a wise move. His lectures didn't faze me at sixteen, but when he released me to the consequences of my own actions, I never got away from his words.

"A wise son heareth his father's instruction:
but a scorner heareth not rebuke" (Proverbs 13:1).

38

Three Dollars

"That's three dollars I wasn't going to make."
Papaw

Papaw was never rich, but for a man who had to eat possums growing up, he did very well financially. Almost none of the money he made ever came in huge lump sums. The only time in his life I can remember him making more than a few dollars at a time was in his later years, when he sold some timber off mountain land. Even that timber sale wasn't huge.

Papaw made his money on an hourly wage, growing livestock, planting tobacco, and doing security work as a constable. The key to him having a home and providing for his family was time management and incremental savings. This is a plan that can work for just about everyone.

We had a disagreement one day over an odd job on the farm. If memory serves me correctly, we were taking used nails out of old boards and straightening them to use again. I hated this tedious work! It seemed like a waste of time to me. The teenager in me just wanted to finish up for the day and go do something else. I decided to enlighten Papaw on the matter, so I told him if you took our time into account, we wouldn't be making three dollars per hour. To which he responded, *"That's three dollars I wasn't going to make."* Checkmate. In Papaw's thinking, there was no other activity at the moment to make more money, so $3 was the best thing going.

Not every person is going to have a large salary job. Large chunks of cash through real estate transactions or cryptocurrency investments are not in the future of most young people. But every young person can incrementally be better off financially if they'll be good stewards over little things. The old man did well for himself. Other old men, following the same pattern, did well too.

"And he said unto him, Well, thou good servant: because thou hast been faithful in a very little, have thou authority over ten cities" (Luke 19:17).

39

Organization

"Put my stuff back where it belongs."
Dad

Dad was intent on taking good care of anything that belonged to him, and he was intent on keeping his things organized. This was especially true about his tools. Dad, like others of his generation, was a fan of Sears Craftsman tools. They were well-made and had a lifetime warranty. If a Craftsman wrench broke, which was unlikely, all you had to do was walk into Sears and hand them the broke wrench, and they handed you a new one. Dad was well-stocked with Craftsman tools which were organized into a large toolbox.

Other tools were also well organized. Everything had a place, and everything stayed in its place. Period. No exceptions. Dad really didn't like me messing with his stuff, but if I did, it was expected that I would put it back where it belonged.

Dad worked on his own vehicles until they became too electronically complicated for him to do so. He changed his own oil and did his own brakes. He was an efficient worker who didn't like to waste time looking for tools. He knew exactly which tool he needed, and he knew exactly where it was supposed to be located. This was his way. These were his tools, and it was his life being wasted if they were out of place. If you lose a tool, it has to be purchased again, and that's a waste of life and resources.

Organization is important. Some things can't be neatly organized in life. Life often takes us out of a normal routine and makes a neat, organized plan impossible. It's also true that much of life is left in our hands to do with it as we choose. Organized, disciplined people are far more efficient and productive than non-organized people.

"He becometh poor that dealeth with a slack hand: but the hand of the diligent maketh rich" (Proverbs 10:4).

40

Leaving Things Better Than You Found Them

"If you borrow something, take it back in better shape than you got it."
Dad

East Tennessee farmers were not normally wealthy people. As they transitioned from using mules and horses to using tractors and tractor-implements, they couldn't afford to buy every needed implement available. So, they often borrowed implements back and forth depending on who owned certain things. This arrangement allowed folks to have the advantage of more efficient equipment without having to go into debt for it. Neighbors helped one another.

Dad really didn't like borrowing anything, but necessity often called for it. Dad's golden rule of borrowing anything was this, *"If you borrow something, take it back in better shape than you got it."* Dad was highly respected by everyone for how he took care of things. If your equipment needed cleaning, he'd clean it. If it needed greased, he'd grease it. If something on it was malfunctioning, he'd fix it if possible.

I have personally tried to carry Dad's philosophy about borrowing equipment into the relationship I have with people. For example, if I'm invited by another pastor to preach to his congregation, my goal is to leave that church in better shape than I found it. This is also my goal every Sunday morning when I get in the pulpit at the church I pastor. I want anyone who attends to go home in better shape than when they came. And I hope I can do this in personal relationships also. If each of us sought to better the lives of other people, the world would be an awesome place. The old man had no idea his insistence on respecting his neighbor's things would influence my ministry, but it has. People should be better by just knowing us.

"The Lord give mercy unto the house of Onesiphorus; for he oft refreshed me, and was not ashamed of my chain" (II Timothy 1:16).

41

Moonshine and Murder

"They killed my brothers."
Papaw

Papaw was an elected constable. He spent years tracking down moonshiners and illegal liquor stills in the mountains. He hated alcohol with a passion. His hatred of the illegal liquor trade was well-founded.

When asked about his obsession with busting stills, he'd say, *"They killed my brothers."* Papaw lost three family members in alcohol-related deaths. One brother had his head blown off with a shotgun. Another brother had his throat cut from ear to ear. A young nephew drowned in his own vomit while drunk.

Today, many have a romantic, favorable view of moonshiners and moonshine. This view is not based on the reality of all the devastation liquor brought into the Appalachians. Moonshine was the meth of its day! Moonshiners were the meth dealers of their day. Poverty is often used as an excuse for those who made and distributed illegal liquor. It ought to be stated that the majority of mountain people hated moonshine, and the evil it caused in their communities!

Alcohol is brain poison to me. One of the greatest frauds in history is how the liquor companies have convinced men that being a man involves alcohol. Alcohol has never made any man a better man, but it has made plenty of men into lesser men. And it has never helped a boy become a man.

Although I knew better, I had a period in my life where I gave alcohol a try. I nearly killed one of my best friends one night because of it, and I endangered my own life more than once while drinking. I thank God, He delivered me from it. The old man was right about liquor.

My advice to young men is this: *Never drink a drop of alcohol!*

"Wine is a mocker, strong drink is raging: and whosoever is deceived thereby is not wise" (Proverbs 20:1).

Berry Tarlton with a load of confiscated moonshine.

42

Guns Are Not Toys

"Never pull a gun on a man unless you plan to use it."
Dad & Papaw

Dad and Papaw had several firearms. They had revolvers, pistols, shotguns and rifles. They were not target shooters or the kind of men who enjoyed shooting just to be shooting. Both were in law enforcement. They were hunters, and they were men who would defend their family if needed. Guns were not a hobby to them. Guns were not toys to them. Guns were tools. Killing tools.

Papaw and Dad taught me to respect firearms at an early age. They drilled it into my head, over and over, that guns had to be handled with caution. Although the state of Tennessee required hunter safety, I really didn't need the class. Everything I needed to know about basic hunting and safety had already been passed down to me by the old men.

Both of them at different times and using differing phraseologies said to me something like this, *"Never pull a gun on a man unless you intend to use it."* Guns are not to be used as threats in the real world. In reference to people, a gun should never be drawn unless it is a life-or-death situation. If you use a gun as a threat and don't intend to use it, the perceived threat may actually use their firearm to kill you. I was taught that a gun was something you only pull if life is at stake, and if you pull it, you use it. Thankfully, I've never had to defend my life with a firearm. I hope I never do.

Boys need to be taught the proper handling and use of firearms. They need to know how to hunt and kill for food. They need to be prepared to defend their own life and someday their families. Handling firearms safely and effectively is essential knowledge. The old men have always known this.

"And he took his staff in his hand and chose him five smooth stones out of the brook and put them in a shepherd's bag which he had, even in a scrip; and his sling was in his hand: and he drew near to the Philistine" (I Samuel 17:40).

TL Jones and his horse Gypsy around the
time of his conversion to Christ.

TL Jones and the beagle.

TL, Terry Jones & Berry Tarlton.

T.L. Jones & his son Benjamin.

Berry Tarlton - the night he was inducted into the
Tennessee Bear Hunters Hall of Fame.

Hannah Jones, Terry Jones and Benjamin Jones.

Jane Jones, Terry Jones & TL.

Jim Holt

Lloyd Tarlton, Denver Tarlton, Bulow Cutshaw & Berry Tarlton.
October 1954.

Pine Springs Missionary Baptist Church -
The author was saved here in 1989.

The mountains where our people live, worship and hunt.

Terry Jones & his granddaughter Hannah Barnes on her wedding day.

Terry Jones with his granddaughter Lydia Price and great granddaughter Carolina Jones.

Terry Jones, Berry Tarlton & Benjamin Jones.

The house where Terry Jones was raised.

TL's grandchildren
Carolina Jones, Sadie Barnes, Hattie Price and Jeb Barnes.

Terry Jones and his grandson Kase.

43

Reality is Undefeated

"I've got a .44 magnum at the house."
Dad

R eality is undefeated. Let me say that again. *Reality is undefeated.* No amount of fantasy, well wishes, illusions or misplaced hopes have any chance of turning back the relentless power of reality. Unfortunately, too many folks throughout world history have erroneously thought they could challenge reality and come out the winner. Every last person who has sought to live a life or make decisions contrary to reality has suffered for it.

Dad began his career in county law enforcement working in the jail. He met all kinds of men there. One disillusioned inmate was infatuated with himself. According to him, he had been shot a couple of times and thought he was invincible. He bragged that no gun could kill him. Dad wasn't one for nonsense. He responded to the inmate's boasting by saying, *"I've got a .44 magnum at the house, and I promise you if I shot you with it, you'd die."* Dad wasn't making threats. He was stating a fact. If the right person shoots you in the right place, with the right firearm, you're going to die. That's reality. No amount of experience, bragging or well-wishing will change that reality. I'm not sure if the inmate realized it or not, but Dad was doing him a favor.

No matter the subject, it's best to know the truth. Facing reality is not always easy, because it often falls outside our notions or desires. We need to face reality concerning God, ourselves and eternity. We need to accept reality concerning how we live in this world, and the obvious consequences of both sin and faith. Believing something doesn't make it true. Not believing something doesn't make it false. Being sincerely wrong is still wrong. Truth is absolute. Reality is undefeated.

"Jesus saith unto him, I am the way, the truth, and the life: no man cometh unto the Father, but by me" (John 14:6).

44

Tough Love

"Set down and shut up".
Papaw

Papaw and I had a great relationship. He loved me, and I loved him. There was mutual respect between us. We were buddies. However, it was always understood he was my elder, and I was the child. We could talk about most anything, but I knew there was a line in our relationship that I wasn't to cross. That line was any type of disrespect concerning his authority in my life. He was not an authoritarian. He wasn't a control freak of any sort. In fact, he offered me opportunities to do things other adults wouldn't have allowed.

Only one time in our relationship did I cross that line of disrespect in such a way he felt the need to discipline me. He watched the news on TV every night, religiously. He counted on Walter Cronkite to tell him what was going on in the world. He lived in an isolated rural valley in the mountains of East Tennessee but was seriously interested in world events. While he watched the news, he expected everyone in the house to be quiet enough for him to hear.

Basketball season was in for my grade school team, and I was running around in the living room jumping up and down trying to touch something that was hanging from the ceiling. I was making too much noise for him to hear. He calmly asked me to settle down. Ignoring him completely, I continued to jump up and down. A man his age considered my behavior unacceptable. He was a gentle man and seldom raised his voice, but on that night, he yelled, *"Set down and shut up."* That shook me. It had never happened before, and my immediate response was to yell back, "You shut up." The line was crossed. He stood up and spanked me without another word being spoken. He went back to his seat, and I remained quiet. He solidified on my butt and in my brain that disrespect to that extent wasn't up for debate.

It was the only time in my life he yelled at me, and it was the only time he ever spanked me. I never gave him a reason to discipline me again. It wasn't really because I was afraid of another spanking. He was so good to me; I didn't want to disappoint him. I'd crossed a reasonably established line. The discipline was deserved. Allowing a child to disrespect elders has no good outcome for them in life. The Bible actually refers to discipline as love. The old man loved me even if it required tough love.

"He that spareth his rod hateth his son: but he that loveth him chasteneth him betimes" (Proverbs 13:24).

45

Noise

"Turn the radio off."
Dr. Darrell Champlin (Missionary)

Dr. Darrell Champlin was a Christian missionary to remote, dangerous areas in Africa and South America. He was an incredible man. I first met him during my first year of college. Later I spent some time with him in South America observing his mission work.

During one of his lectures, he addressed the topic of noise. Specifically, he warned that American Christians had so much noise in their lives, it was impeding them from hearing the voice of God. Meditating on God's Word takes undistracted listening. Any noise that disrupts our ability to hear God is bad for us, no matter what the noise is. Modern man seems to be uncomfortable alone in silence.

Do you ever sit in the silence of your own thoughts? Thinking in silence is a lost art. Meditation is a lost art. Dr. Champlin lived and ministered in dangerous places. Some of the people in the area he lived in wanted him dead. He needed to know God. He needed

God's direction. The old missionary was right. It's beneficial in life for us to turn off noise at times and just listen to that still small voice of God.

"Be still and know that I am God: I will be exalted among the heathen, I will be exalted in the earth" (Psalm 46:10).

46

Reverence

*"Do you think God would be upset
if we baled hay today?"*
Dad

D ad grew up in a transitional generation. He was born in 1947, and the old mountain folks were very traditional regarding religious matters. One of the things you didn't do in Appalachia on Sunday was "work." Years ago, almost everything was closed in rural America on Sunday. Sunday was sacred to the old timers because it was viewed as a day of worship.

Traditional values were seriously challenged during the sexual revolution of the 1960's. The public's reverence for Sunday as the Lord's Day began to be disregarded. By the 2000's only the most religious Christians gave any thought to Sunday as a special day of any kind. In Appalachia, some of the old ways still existed in the heart of the older generations. Papaw and Dad, to their dying day, held Sunday in high regard. Papaw wouldn't even hunt on Sunday. Dad would hunt or work at the Sheriff's office, but nothing he considered unnecessary. Papaw limited his work basically to feeding the stock.

As Dad died slowly with Scleroderma, toward the end of his life, he grew weaker and weaker, but he didn't stop farming. One week he had mowed some hay and needed to get it up before the rain came. Because of his sickness, he was limited in certain ways and needed help. After one Sunday morning service he asked me, *"Do you think God would be upset if we baled hay today?"* If you know the Bible, you know God makes certain provisions for emergency situations. It's OK to get your ox out of a ditch no matter what day it is or isn't. However, Dad considered Sunday with a great deal of reverence. His people before him did as well. The entire nation once felt this way. I assured him that getting that hay up under the circumstances would be just fine.

When we got to the hayfield, Dad climbed up in a John Deere cab tractor and prepared to bale. I was assigned to a smaller Ford tractor and was going to rake the hay in front of him. Just as I was about to step up on the tractor, I was flooded with gratitude. I fell to my knees beside that tractor, and with tears streaming down my face, I thanked God I was raised in a family that had reverence for the things of God. I was in my 40's, and it was the first time in my life that Dad and I had farmed together on a Sunday.

You can debate days of worship and traditions all you want, but there's something good to be said about a people who have a reverence for God that lives so deeply within them. In a world where so many have no standards or reverence at all for anything, I'm never going to criticize those who do. As our society crumbles around us, it might pay us to reconsider why the older generation took certain things so seriously.

"Now when Jesus was risen early the first day of the week, he appeared first to Mary Magdalene, out of whom he had cast seven devils" (Mark 16:9).

47

Room to Roam

"Son, you go right ahead and do anything you want."
Uncle Tom

My grandparents owned a good-sized farm, but they didn't live on it. They lived about ten miles away from their farm on a small parcel of ground my Mamaw had been gifted by her Momma. Their property joined land owned by Mamaw's brother. He was my great uncle. Uncle Tom's farm backed up to the Cherokee National Forest on both sides of State Highway 107.

I could easily walk to the Cherokee National Forest in less than ten minutes in either direction, but to get there, somebody's private property had to be crossed. Uncle Tom was a benevolent man. Every time I'd ask for permission to do something on his farm or cross his property to get to government land, he'd say something like, *"Son, you go right ahead and do anything you want."* My cousin and I squirrel hunted on Uncle Tom's land. Papaw and I shot frogs out of Uncle Tom's pond. We both loved fried frog legs. I'd go up to a certain hollow where Uncle Tom dumped trash and shoot all sorts of stuff, just for fun. I shot a TV up there once, and the explosion of that old Magnavox TV tube was awesome! As long as I wasn't tearing anything up or hurting myself, I was free to explore, play and hunt.

Across the road from my grandparents, my great Uncle Hobert owned a farm. He was just like Uncle Tom with me regarding hunting permission. He didn't care one bit. All through that mountain valley were kinfolks and neighbors who treated me like gold. I could do just about anything I wanted, and those old folks loved to know I was enjoying myself. I had some of the best times of my childhood roaming and hunting those farms and the wild places beyond them. I had thousands and thousands of acres to roam. Nobody scolded me. Nobody yelled at me. Nobody cussed me, and nobody called the law on me. The old men loved seeing the boys being boys. Boys need room to roam. And they need the adults around them to want them to roam and explore. The old folks who were so good to me are fondly remembered.

"And the boys grew: and Esau was a cunning hunter, a man of the field; and Jacob was a plain man, dwelling in tents" (Genesis 25:27).

Berry Tarlton & Uncle Tom Shipley

48

Liars

"Don't lie to me."
Dad

Before Dad became a law enforcement officer, he spent several years driving semi-trucks. One company he worked for was a moving company. Dad would go with a crew of men to the customer's home and prepare everything for the move. Then he went back with a truck and trailer and loaded everything up and moved it to whatever designation was assigned to him.

I was probably ten to twelve years old when he invited me to go to a home in a nearby city and help prepare a family's belongings for a cross country haul. During the course of that day, I was given the task of sweeping the kitchen. As I swept, I carelessly hit a low hanging light with the broom handle and broke it. I panicked. I didn't want to be in trouble, so I swept up the broken pieces and put them in the trash.

The next day I declined when I was invited to go back for another day's work. Later that night, when Dad came home from work, he confronted me with the problem I'd hoped would go unnoticed. The homeowners had discovered the broken light and blamed me. Dad, as most parents do, defended me. He told them if his son had broken that light he would've told him. Now, standing in front of him, he very sternly said, *"Don't lie to me."*

Dad hated lying with a red-hot passion. If I did something I wasn't supposed to, or if I broke something, the best policy, with Dad, was always to just confess it immediately. He may be mad or disappointed, but if you were honest, he was going to show mercy. If you lied and got caught lying, there was no mercy.

I confessed to breaking the light. He understood it was an accident. His disappointment in my attempted cover up wasn't passed over lightly. He was deeply embarrassed that he had defended me to his customers, and he knew he'd have to pay for the broken light. There was no reason for him to discipline me any further than that conversation. I already hated what I had done to Dad.

Dad's hatred of lying was a tremendous asset to me. God is truth. Satan is the father of lies. Although Dad wasn't a spiritually minded man when I was that young, he had some God-fearing principles in his heart. Lying is serious business in the Bible. *Children have to be taught not to become liars.* The consequences in life and eternity are too serious.

"Lying lips are abomination to the LORD: but they that deal truly are his delight" (Proverbs 12:22).

Becoming Useful

"All that horse needs is a trip to Cold Springs."
Dad

The maternal side of Dad's family had the last name of Reaves. The Reaves clan were horse people. Of all God's creatures, the horse was Dad's favorite. A lot of his best childhood memories involved horses. It was obvious they brought joy to a young boy who didn't have the easiest of lives. He often referred to the progress of humanity being directly related to the usefulness of horses.

Among horse people, there's a lot of respect for those who can take an unbroken colt and develop it into a useful animal. The old timers expected their stock to earn its keep. They had to scratch from daylight to dawn just to survive, and no animal was going to be given room and board who didn't return some type of value to the family. The poor mountain people didn't have the resources to keep something that eats as much as a horse for a pasture ornament.

If someone had an unbroken horse, especially one with an ornery streak, Dad would often say, *"All that horse needs is a trip to Cold Springs."* Cold Springs was a place in the high country where locals liked to visit. There are names on gravestones there from the Civil War. It's uphill nearly all the way there. A horse who begins the trip to Cold Springs may start out froggy, but on the way there, the long uphill pull takes the sap out of him. Once that horse is worn down, he begins to pay attention and learn some things he normally would've ignored. *Wet saddle blankets make good horses.* A useful horse is a valuable horse.

If you want to be valuable in this world, you need to be useful. Don't concentrate on being special. Your Momma will think you're special just because you are her child. The rest of the world isn't your Momma. They want to know what value you can add to humanity by what you can actually do. You'll need some education, and your education will need to be developed into a skill set that is valued by people who are willing to exchange money for it. Learn to weld. Learn to cook. Learn accounting. Learn to change a tire. Become useful.

A horse that can't be worked or ridden was a liability to a mountain family. A useful horse that could plow a crop, pull a buggy to church or carry a grown man hunting was valuable. Getting and developing skills will require some hard work. You need trips to Cold Springs. Becoming useful isn't easy, but it's far easier than going through life useless.

> *"Then wrought Bezaleel and Aholiab, and every wise hearted man, in whom the LORD put wisdom and understanding to know how to work all manner of work for the service of the sanctuary, according to all that the LORD had commanded" (Exodus 36:1).*

Dad's Blessing

"Are you sure?"
Dad

Dad and I didn't talk a lot. He was a man of few words. I actually didn't really know how to relate to him in some ways. One subject that we did talk about during my teen years was my future in reference to work. He was genuinely interested in what I was going to do after high school. We talked about many options including the military, college or a trade. He was always supportive in the discussion. I knew he wanted me to do well in life. Every Dad wants his son to succeed. I'd say most dads want their sons to do better than them.

I became a Christian in April of 1989. Within a year or so, I began to feel that God had plans for my life in His service. There was no way I could really explain that to anyone at the time. I'm sure I didn't understand all that meant either. I talked to few folks about it. I talked to my mom, who was supportive. I talked to my Great Uncle Joe Tarlton, who seemed to know God was calling me even before I did, and possibly had conversations with a couple other preachers, but that's about it.

When God confirmed to me that I was definitely being called to the ministry, I decided I would share that call with my church on a particular Sunday. The day before I was going to make a public announcement, Dad and I were bear hunting in North Carolina. When the hunt was over, Dad and I were coming out of the mountains in his old Bronco down a road on Big Creek. I looked over at Dad as he slowly drove and told him that God had called me to preach, and that I was going to tell the church publicly the next morning. He looked at me and soberly asked, *"Are you sure?"* I said, "Yes." That was the end of the discussion, and I think we drove home in silence. At the time Dad wasn't a Christian and rarely attended church, but he respected God and his Word.

The next morning after service, just before the congregation was dismissed, I walked to the front of the little mountain church and asked to say a word. When I looked back into the crowd there sat both mom and dad. The church was elated that God had called one of their own to ministry. The entire church lined up to shake my hand. My parents stood in line with everyone waiting their turn to approach me. When Dad stepped up to me, there were tears rolling down his wrinkled face. He leaned over and hugged me, but I don't remember him saying a word. It's the only memory I have of him hugging me as a son growing up. My mom was the physically affectionate parent. I knew that Dad was putting his blessing on my decision. Although I didn't know it, he told others all the time how proud he was I was a preacher. He later became a Christian and would eventually be a member of the church I pastored. He loved to hear me preach. Words are not always necessary. Hugs are not always necessary. But a boy needs his dad's approval. They need to know their dads are proud of them. *The old man's blessing that Sunday is one of my favorite memories.*

> *"And I thank Christ Jesus our Lord, who hath enabled me, for that he counted me faithful, putting me into the ministry"(I Timothy 1:12).*

51

Humility

"I really have a lot of respect for your dad."
Donald "Buck" Sandstrom

Donald Sandstrom, better known as "Buck," is my father-in-law. The first time I ever talked to him was when I called to ask for permission to marry his daughter. We hit it off right from the start and became close friends over time. Some people don't seem to care for their in-laws, but mine are the best.

Buck and my dad have a lot in common. They grew up without a dad present in their lives. Poverty was a way of life for them in their childhood. Neither one of them was afraid of a fight and held the respect of other men in their communities. Buck and Dad both fought for their country in the jungles of Vietnam. Buck was in the infantry and saw a great deal of combat. It's no secret that both of them were rowdy as young men, but they later became Christians and church men. Until retirement, they both worked like borrowed mules to feed their families. Buck worked for the town of West Union, West Virginia, and people depended on Buck when things needed to be taken care of in town. Buck and Dad were men of great common sense and didn't care for foolishness in serious matters. They were, and Buck still is, the kind of men that built America.

I share those comparisons between Buck and Dad so that I can illustrate one of Buck's strongest traits. Many times, over the years, Buck said to me, *"I really respect your dad."* And he often commented on it being an honor for him to know Dad and Papaw. Buck is every bit the man they were but bragged on them instead of himself. That's called humility. Humility is in low quantities today. Men who've accomplished very little in life incessantly boast about nothing. Buck, who has been a man among men, is more likely to brag on someone else he respects. *Real men know real men when they see them.* Real men have little regard for pretenders. But rare is the accomplished man who will esteem others greater than himself. Humility is a tremendous attribute. Boys need to be encouraged to be real men that can appreciate other men and say so. A man who can't see good things in other men and say so is a small man.

"Let another man praise thee, and not thine own mouth; a stranger, and not thine own lips" (Proverbs 27:2).

Buck Sandstrom & his granddaughter Lydia Price

52

Buy Books

*"Buy books now because someday
you'll be buying diapers."*
Dr. David Baughan (Evangelist)

I had a professor in college that was a noted Baptist historian. He was a tremendous man with common sense and book smarts. He routinely recommended to his younger students, *"Buy books now because someday you'll be buying diapers."*

Dr. Baughan was attempting to kill two birds with one stone. He wanted to encourage the importance of being well-read while giving his students practical advice about building a personal library. A mechanic needs tools. A barber needs tools. A farrier needs tools. Books are the tools of the thinking man.

Nobody knows everything. Books give you the ability to learn the wisdom of thousands of men with very little effort. Books are a way to access knowledge otherwise unavailable to you. Not all books are useful. In fact, some books contain pure evil. Dr. Baughan wasn't recommending indiscriminate buying or reading of random, useless books. In particular, he was pointing young preachers toward reading books that would help them be better servants in their calling. The discipline of reading is extremely helpful in life, especially if you buy and read the right books.

Reading isn't just for bookworms or nerds. Reading should be viewed as an essential part of becoming a man who can function effectively in the world in which he lives. The old professor helped us with that humorous advice.

"Till I come, give attendance to reading, to exhortation, to doctrine" (I Timothy 4:13).

53

Restoration and a Guilty Conscience

"I never thought you'd do something like that."
Kenneth Collins

Way too early in life, I developed a taste for chewing tobacco. Around here the word "tobacco" was modified to "baccer." A large percentage of folks in East Tennessee either smoked, chewed, or dipped. It seems wild now but even my public high school had a designated place outside for students to use tobacco.

The problem of wanting tobacco before you're old enough to get a job is that it's hard to get. You're basically dependent on other people to give it to you, or you scrape together nickels and dimes here and there. There is another way to get something that you can't pay for. You can steal it. I'm ashamed to admit it, but on one occasion, this is how I acquired some.

Early one morning, I was heading bear hunting with my Papaw when we stopped by Cove Creek Market. Cove Creek Market was owned by Kenneth Collins who was a family friend. Kenneth was a hard-working, kind man. He was about the last store owner left in our area that wouldn't sell alcohol in his store.

As Papaw talked to Kenneth, I was eyeing the tobacco rack. My cravings were stronger than my morals that morning, and I devised a plan. I wandered around behind the tobacco rack and got down on my knees on the floor. This put me out of sight of both Papaw and Kenneth, who were talking. I slipped my hand into the tobacco rack and swiped a pouch of Redman. Then I eased to the back corner of the store into the bathroom where I concealed the tobacco.

Years passed, and I never told anyone that I stole from our family friend. When I was eighteen, I became a Christian, and within a few years, God called me into the ministry. I spent four years in college and two years serving as a youth pastor in Virginia. Then I moved my family to Montana where we started a new church. After laboring two years in Montana, we made a trip back east to visit family and take care of some ministry business. I had forgotten about stealing from Mr. Collins, but God had not forgotten.

During our trip home, I passed Kenneth's home on the way to my grandparents. The Lord reached way down into my conscience and reminded me that I had stolen from that man, and it needed to be repaid. God had forgiven me of my sin of stealing, but there was a matter of restoration that I had never settled up. A thief can be forgiven, but God expects them to restore what they've stolen. My guilty conscience took the steering wheel and pulled my vehicle into Kenneth's driveway. By this time Kenneth had sold the store and had retired. That didn't matter. I owed him at least one pack of Redman tobacco and interest.

The walk up to Kenneth's door was a long walk. Thankfully, he was home and greeted me at the door. He was thrilled to see me. The old folks, where I grew up, really did love the kids in the community and supported our success. They especially loved to see a kid serve the Lord. I got straight to the point in confessing my sin to Kenneth. His response was a dagger to the heart. Very softly, he said, *"I never thought you'd do something like that."* Man, that hurt. He knew my Papaw and Dad wouldn't steal from him, and he was surprised that I had.

Kenneth Collins

I asked him to forgive me, and he instantly granted me forgiveness. Then I offered to make restitution in any way that he saw fit. He was the offended party and had every right to expect that debt to be settled. If he had told me I owed him one hundred dollars, I would've paid him. Instead, he forgave my debt and would not accept any restitution at all. He was exactly the kind of man I remembered him to be.

That was an uncomfortable experience for me. I was embarrassed, but I pulled out of his driveway forgiven. My conscience was clear. If either Dad or Papaw had caught me stealing, it would have been a "Katy, bar the door" moment. Our elders can't see everything we do, but God does. The sins of your youth need forgiveness, and in some cases, you need to make restitution. A clean conscience is the only way to live.

"And Zacchaeus stood, and said unto the Lord; Behold, Lord, the half of my goods I give to the poor; and if I have taken any thing from any man by false accusation, I restore him fourfold" (Luke 19:8).

54

Pulling Your Weight

"If I have to do your job for you, there's no reason for me to pay you to do it."
Dr. John Godfrey (Pastor)

My first ministry just out of college was in Chesapeake, Virginia. Dr. John Godfrey was the senior pastor of Great Hope Baptist Church and my new boss. As soon as I arrived in Chesapeake, I was called to Godfrey's office for an explanation of my responsibilities, a summary of his ministry philosophy, and an assurance of his support. Youth Pastor would be my title, and I understood clearly what the expectations were.

In that first meeting, Pastor Godfrey told me there would be one staff meeting per week. The meeting would be on Wednesday morning for one hour. Everyone on staff sat in his office and took turns sharing ideas and concerns. When the hour ended, the meeting ended. Pastor Godfrey had no interest in long, useless meetings. He further stated, very emphatically, that I was not to be in his office all the time interrupting him. He had his own work to do. Near the end of our introductory discussion, he said, *"If I have to do your job for you, there's no reason for me to pay you to do it."*

I understood Godfrey perfectly. He didn't know it at the time, but I was raised by men who believed in pulling their own weight. The old men in my life weren't perfect, but they did their part. Dad would do his part and more. As I type this, I can see Dad shirtless and in the tobacco field with a rag wrapped around his head to keep the sweat out of his eyes. On his shoulders, he would carry a massive load of tobacco sticks to be laid down in the rows, in preparation for harvesting the tobacco. I never could get the size load on my shoulders that Dad could. Nobody else that helped us could either. Papaw carried his load. My cousins who helped on the farm carried their load. Anybody that Dad hired was expected to carry their load.

When bear hunting in the mountains, certain men were more respected than others. The respect was in relation to the load they carried during the day's hunt. Anyone who shirked their responsibility bear hunting was viewed on a lower plain than the tougher men. Part of becoming a man, a huge part, is pulling your own weight in life. Pastor Godfrey wasn't telling me anything I didn't already know, but the way he said it stuck with me. Today people brag about being shirkers. That kind of attitude comes from men who will never accomplish anything great or difficult in life. Little men leave the hardest jobs to the best of men. The old pastor was singing the same tune with different lyrics. Whatever a boy's size, expect him to pull his weight, and let the weight increase as he does. Give him the shovel that fits him and expect him to get a full shovel load.

"Then I told them of the hand of my God which was good upon me; as also the king's words that he had spoken unto me. And they said, Let us rise up and build. So they strengthened their hands for this good work" (Nehemiah 2:18).

55

Leopard's Spots

"If I could get down on my knees, I'd get down there and pray with you."
Doyle Reaves

Dad didn't have a present father figure in his life. His dad ran off when he was two and lived up north somewhere. Several old men in Dad's family and community filled in the gap in what ways they could. These old men were special to Dad, and he spoke of them often.

One of the men who took Dad under his wings, in certain ways, was his Uncle Doyle Reaves. Uncle Doyle was the man who stepped in when Grandaddy Jones fled up north. He gathered the material and built them a small home to live in on the Reaves family farm. Uncle Doyle stories were commonplace with Dad. Stories about horses, camping, farming and some rough living. Uncle Doyle was known for his salty language.

After I became a Christian, the Lord put a real burden on my heart for my great uncles. They were good to me, but several of them had made it into their later years away from God. I was never close to Uncle Doyle, but I had met him a few times. Dad got us a Boston terrier pup from him once, and I took him a mess of fish when I was a teenager. Even though I wasn't personally close to him, he mattered to me, because he had mattered so much to Dad. He was a lynch pin in a little boy's life when he needed a man.

I determined that I was going go tell Uncle Doyle about Jesus. Grandmother Jones, Uncle Doyle's sister, warned me that I was in for rude treatment. She said he would just cuss me for coming over there. Nevertheless, I was bound to go. It wouldn't be the first cussing I ever took.

When I knocked on his door, he yelled for me to "come on in." He had no clue who I was but wasn't feeling well enough to come to the door. Once he knew I was "Terry's boy," everything was fine. Much of my life has been that way. When people find out who my family is, the doors are opened. I'm thankful for that.

I'm not one for much jibber jabber. For someone who's called to pastor, I'm woefully ill- equipped with small talk. Maybe I would get cussed, but I dove right into talking to Uncle Doyle about his need for a Savior.

I was blindsided by his response. He told me that a few weeks prior to my visit, he had had a heart attack and was hauled by ambulance to town. During the ride, the fear of dying overwhelmed him, and he called on the Lord Jesus to save him. He went on to explain that he had been watching Billy Graham preach the gospel on TV, and when the heart attack struck, he knew it was time to get right with God. The old rough neck was gentle as a lamb as we talked. When I offered to pray for him, he said, *"If I could get down on my knees, I'd get down there and pray with you."*

Uncle Doyle hadn't told anyone about his conversion. Dad and Grandmother were surprised by it too. He passed away not long after my visit, and I'm sure much of the family just assumed he had gone to Hell unrepentant. I had the privilege of telling them Uncle Doyle was certainly with Jesus. Jesus can forgive an old sinner. People can get saved on their death bed. Even if it's the last hour, the last minute, the last second and the last breath, God can save anyone that calls out in faith. The roughest of men can be converted. Being born again is real. A leopard can't change his own spots, but the living God can change a leopard into a lamb.

"Can the Ethiopian change his skin, or the leopard his spots? then may ye also do good, that are accustomed to do evil" (Jeremiah 13:23).

Tim Reaves and Doyle Reaves.

56

Hell & Hypocrisy

"If a preacher believes in Hell, how can he retire?"
Dad

Dad believed every word of the Bible. Papaw believed every word of the Bible. I believe every word of the Bible. We all believe in the pleasant parts about salvation and Heaven and the unpleasant parts about Hell. Even some of the roughest sinners in our family believed the Bible was God's Word.

With very few exceptions, the old mountain people believed in a literal, fiery Hell just as Jesus taught and was recorded in the Bible. Mothers with lost, non-Christian children prayed for them with tears. The worst thing, in all of life, was to believe someone you loved died without Jesus and went to Hell! Any preacher who denied the reality of a literal Hell would have been scorned completely as an apostate.

Dad and I were on our way home from a dove hunt when we passed the parsonage of a church. The pastor who lived there had recently retired. That confused Dad. He asked me, *"If a preacher believes in Hell, how can he retire?"* What a question! It's possible to get too feeble to pastor a congregation, but there's no way a man who truly believes in Hell could ever stop preaching the gospel and loaf the rest of his life away. I think that pastor's retirement rattled Dad. He had respected that pastor for years. Now, he was wondering if that pastor had been a hypocrite all the time.

Dad didn't accuse the pastor of being a hypocrite. He only asked a question that would obviously lead to a similar conclusion, if true, in the sense that Dad saw it. If Hell is real, you can't stop trying to keep people from going there just because you're old enough to draw social security. Dad had the utmost respect for preachers. He held them in high esteem. It was just on this one day, he couldn't grasp retirement in light of Hell. There's a lot to consider when it comes to Dad's question, but the one thing I took from it was this – a preacher's life should reflect his preaching. People will look over a lot of inconsistencies in preachers. No rational person believes a preacher can be perfect. But the one thing that will undermine a preacher's credibility is blatant hypocrisy. The old man's question was simple but powerful.

"And fear not them which kill the body, but are not able to kill the soul: but rather fear him which is able to destroy both soul and body in hell" (Matthew 10:28).

57

Bar Fights

"No fair! No fair! Hitting in the ear!"
Dale Peyton

My wife has an uncle named Dale Peyton. Uncle Dale and I spent a lot of time together one fall, deer hunting in West Virginia. He's one of my favorite people to talk to because he has some unique perspectives on life, and he's always blatantly honest with how he sees things. He's a master storyteller and weaves reality and humor together in a way that makes you want to listen to everything he says.

Dale was pretty rowdy in his younger days and had a lot of experiences in places where crazy stuff happened. I can't tell a story the way Uncle Dale does, so I won't even try. One night Dale was at a bar, and a fight broke out between two men. During the fight, one of the men yelled, *"No fair! No fair! Hitting in the ear!"* That's a wild thing to yell during a bar fight because everyone knows that in the real world, fights have no weight limits, no time limits and no referees. Outside of organized sanctioned fights, like you see in MMA or boxing, it's every-man-for-himself and no-holds-barred.

Every boy needs to know how to fight. We live in a dangerous world, and knowing how to defend yourself isn't an option. Most American boys in 2024 are ill-equipped to handle business in a real fight. They have no concept of all that happens when there are no rules and no referees.

Mostly, they need to be taught how to stay out of places and away from people who needlessly end up in fights. Boys shouldn't be cowards, and they also shouldn't be mindless idiots in reference to violence. You can be the toughest man in the world and get sucker- punched. You can be the bravest man in the neighborhood and make some coward mad, and he'll pull out a gun and shoot you. Papaw used to say, "You don't have to fear a brave man. They face you. You have to fear cowards because they sneak up and shoot you." Just being in the wrong place, at the wrong time, with the wrong people could put you in an early grave.

Dale Peyton.

Let me make it plain for those of who who've lived sheltered lives. We live in a world with dangerous people. If you get yourself into a predicament with one of those people it's not like MMA, boxing, or high school wrestling. You can get stabbed, shot, or have your brains beat out with a bar stool. Playing Mr. Tough Guy is like Russian Roulette. It's just a matter of time before you run up on the wrong dude. Or run up on a little weasel-of-a-coward who hurts you from behind. You're living among people who have no rules, and you can't operate by your rules in their environment. The old men have a million experiences. They'll help you if you listen with an ear to hear the important part of the story.

"And Ehud put forth his left hand, and took the dagger from his right thigh, and thrust it into his belly" (Judges 3:21).

58

Choosing Leaders

*"Anybody strong enough to help you
is strong enough to hurt you."*
Dr. John Godfrey (Pastor)

W hen Pastor John Godfrey hired me to serve as the youth pastor of Great Hope Baptist Church, he had no idea what he was getting. The college I graduated from recommended me, and we had a brief in-person interview. I was hired on the spot.

In our first few days in ministry together, he wanted to make sure we were on the same page. Unfortunately, it's not uncommon for young men coming onto staff in local churches to become more of a problem than they are an asset. Men straight out of college often know just enough to be dangerous. They have knowledge but haven't lived long enough to apply their knowledge appropriately. Some of them go entirely rogue, attempting to build a ministry within a ministry, which has the potential to cause a church split. Good senior pastors want someone strong enough to lead but humble enough to follow. Pastor Godfrey, in his own words, explained it this way to me. *"Anyone strong enough to help you is strong enough to hurt you."* I understood.

Throughout my ministry, that advice has been extremely helpful as I've chosen leaders for various departments within the two churches I've started and pastored. Spiritual leaders must be servants first, so I look for people who will do the work that needs to be done without a title or position. I observe my church folks to see if they do simple things like picking up gum wrappers off the floor just because it needs doing. I'm also curious about their willingness to receive and follow instruction. If they have a servants' heart and are good followers, there is a fundamental basis for them to also lead. If they will not serve and will not follow, I'll never consider them for a position or give them a title. I don't want to know if you'll boss people around, I want to know if you'll clean the toilets without expecting a blue ribbon.

Those who exhibit a servant's heart and follow instruction are generally good material for leadership. Finding leaders is really simple. Watch to see if others will follow them. Leaders have to be self-starters, have to have strong convictions and rhinoceros hide. This toughness has to be accompanied by a love for people and tempered by grace. These kinds of people in a church are strong enough to help you but will have no interest in hurting you. The old preacher knew what he was saying on leadership. It's hard telling how much that one piece of advice has helped me the past twenty-five plus years.

"Only be thou strong and very courageous, that thou mayest observe to do according to all the law, which Moses my servant commanded thee: turn not from it to the right hand or to the left, that thou mayest prosper whithersoever thou goest" (Joshua 1:7).

59

Vietnam

"I don't know. Let me know what you find out."
Dad

From the time I was old enough to think about serious matters, I was curious about Dad's military service in Vietnam. He served in the Army's artillery. Dad passed away several years ago, and I still know very little about his time in the war. He didn't talk about it much. Unlike others, Dad didn't avoid talking about Vietnam because it caused flashbacks or something like that. He just didn't care about it. I would not have known that he had commendation medals, including a Purple Heart, if I had not found them by accident one day.

Here and there, over the years, I picked up bits and pieces. He went to boot camp in Oklahoma at Fort Sill. I know he spent time in Chu Lai, Da Nang and Hue in Vietnam. Helicopters fascinated him and he wanted to learn to fly one. His unit had a lot of boys from the south. The Lieutenant that he served under was a real jerk, and Dad hated him. A Vietcong booby trap exploded, and he was hit by shrapnel in the shoulder and that earned him the Purple Heart. Even though he saw plenty of combat, he never thought he would die in Vietnam. That's about it. He wasn't much on war stories.

When I was in high school, one of my teachers gave a class assignment for us to write some sort of essay. Having been curious about Vietnam for years, I went to Dad for information. He was standing at his work bench in the basement when I asked him what the purpose of Vietnam was all about. He stopped working and looked at me puzzled. I wish I could describe the look on his face. It was like looking at a blank dry erase board. He said, *"I don't know. Let me know what you find out."* Then he refocused and went back to work. That floored me. How can your government draft a country boy to a war in a foreign jungle, allow him to risk his life and force him to watch other American men die, and not even give a good explanation for why he's even there?

According to the Bible, God has ordained human government for a specific reason (Romans 13). Government has a legitimate purpose. Christians are to obey government ordinances so long as they don't require them to sin against God. However, human history is replete with governments abusing their powers. Some of the most horrific crimes the world has ever experienced have been government sanctioned. Some of these atrocities have been perpetrated against their own citizens. Good government is fantastic for humanity. Bad government has proven catastrophic for humanity. Boys need to be taught the balance in this.

Patriotism is a fine thing for good government. A boy ought to love his country and support it, if possible. Many of America's best men have fought and died for our freedoms. Those men deserve our gratitude and respect. Yet as America's founders believed, government should be of the people, by the people, and for the people. It's good to explain to boys that government can go bad, and to have a healthy distrust in even their own government. Politicians are capable of lying. Governments can become corrupt. They will send boys off to die in faraway places for no good reason. Being an American patriot is honorable. Being an educated skeptical patriot is a safeguard to your own liberty. Dad was 100% red, white and blue, but after Vietnam, he lived the rest of his life not even knowing why he was there.

"And he wrote in the letter, saying, Set ye Uriah in the forefront of the hottest battle, and retire ye from him, that he may be smitten, and die" (II Samuel 11:15).

Terry Jones in Vietnam.

60

Guitars & Dreams

"You won't be able to play that guitar."
Dad

Mamaw, my mom's mom, and Grandmother, my dad's mom, were very good to me. Either one of them would've given me the moon, if they would've had it to give. They seldom did anything together, but on one occasion I was with them both in town. I'm not sure what the occasion was. During our trip, I mentioned that I'd like to have a guitar. For some reason, they both liked that idea. Before leaving town, they took me up to the local music store and bought me a boy-sized guitar and case.

Mamaw arranged for me to take guitar lessons from her sister-in-law Edith. Aunt Edith was a fantastic musician who could play multiple instruments. She was more than happy to get me started. I can still remember her taking tape and marking places on that guitar for me to learn chords.

I was so certain of my future success that I immediately started my own band. Being the only member of the band allowed me to choose the name. The inspiration for naming my band came from a black T-shirt I had. On the front of that shirt was a gold sparkly stallion rearing up in all its equine glory. The band would be called "The Golden Stallion" band. Mamaw took some of those old iron-on velvet letters and put the band name just above the stallion. I had a guitar, a band and now I had a logo. Nashville was only four hours and ten years away. I've always been a dreamer.

Dad didn't quite see my vision. His view came from a weird idea he had about the ability to play instruments. He stated it this way, *"You won't be able to play the guitar. That's something that runs in families."* I'm not sure why he believed that playing music was genetic. His words lodged in my little brain. The Gold Stallion band was over before its first gig. Looking back, it's even more strange that Dad held that belief because he had a nice Yamaha guitar that he attempted to play. He picked and sang Tom Dooley over and over. Maybe he gave up the guitar because of the same belief. I don't know.

Dad's belief and words were a dream killer. It's probably for the best, because God had other plans for me besides picking in the Honky Tonks of Nashville. This doesn't change the effect Dad's discouraging words had on me. Words matter. Everything we say to a child matters. I don't share this story to criticize Dad. Anyone that reads my writings will quickly know, he's a hero to me. Yet every boy needs to know even their heroes can be wrong, and every old man needs to know his words matter more than he thinks. Never call a kid stupid. Never tell them they can't. Unless their hopes and dreams are sinful, don't crush their spirit. Build boys that believe they can do anything that God wills for them.

Genetics in some ways does determine what's possible in our lives. Not many short men are going to make millions in the NBA. We all understand that. Yet in areas where hard work and determination can pay off, encourage them to go as high and as far as they can. The dreams of boys have allowed men to build planes and fly. Let the boys dream.

"And they said one to another, Behold, this dreamer cometh" (Genesis 37:19).

61

Commitment

*"If you can't afford a $150 payment,
we need to get out of here."*
Dad

A fter my first truck blew up, I had to have some wheels. A local Nissan dealer placed an ad in *The Greeneville Sun* with a special on two vehicles. For $8,995.00 you could get a Nissan Sentra or a Nissan pickup. I'm a truck man for sure, but the truck in the sale ad was a 2-wheel drive, and that wouldn't have helped me at all. I was driving several miles a day to work and to college, and the gas mileage of the Sentra really appealed to me.

Dad went with me to the dealership to help me navigate the deal. I had never bought a new car, and to this day, I have never bought another one. The salesman laid the paperwork in front of me, and the payment was $153 per month. I was living at home and had a good job at a factory. Money wasn't pouring out of my pockets, but that payment was no big deal to a single guy with no bills.

As I sat there looking at that paperwork, I froze. I became indecisive about whether or not I should buy the car. I needed it. It was affordable. Dad thought it was a good decision.

Something was holding me up. I just hated the idea of a long-term commitment. I had never really fully committed myself to anything long term in writing before. Dad grew frustrated. He was a firm believer in the responsible use of credit. His life had been bettered substantially by borrowing money, working hard and making double payments. Exasperated, he said to me, *"If you can't make a $150 payment, we need to get out of here."* Hesitantly, I pulled the trigger and left in a shiny new car.

We all have faults, and one of mine is indecisiveness at times. I struggle to commit to things, especially if I know it's a long-term commitment. There's nothing wrong with thinking things through and being patient, but there comes a time when you have to go for it. Decisions have to be made. Commitments to long-term matters are associated with some of the best parts of life. Marriage, having children, buying a home, owning a business and a million other things require long-term, or in some cases, lifetime commitments. Those commitments are absolutely worth the rewards that follow them. Committing yourself to the best things of life and following through on those commitments are far better than the non-rewarding alternatives. Dad wasn't trying to deal out life lessons at that dealership. He just wanted to make the deal or get back to work. When boys become men, they stop seeing commitment as some kind of chain that holds them down and start seeing it as a rope to climb to the top of the highest mountains.

"That which is gone out of thy lips thou shalt keep and perform; even a freewill offering, according as thou hast vowed unto the LORD thy God, which thou hast promised with thy mouth" (Deuteronomy 23:23).

1: 62

Quality

2: *"He who rolls up his sleeves seldom loses his shirt."*
Unknown (via Doc Love)

During my high school years, my favorite class was Agricultural Mechanics. The teacher was an older man by the name of Doc Love. I don't know if Doc was his real name or a nickname. He was the only teacher that we called by his first name. Calling an adult by their first name was unusual when I was growing up. Doc was probably in his 70's during my time in high school but was a slender man with plenty of get up and go.

In his classroom, there was a thick picture frame that Doc used to put inspirational quotes on. The only one I remember out of all four years I was in his class read, *"He who rolls up his sleeves seldom loses his shirt."* Doc, like most men of his generation, believed in hard work. What I remember most about Doc was his absolute insistence on *quality* work. Every project Doc assigned was graded based on his personal inspection of the project. He was a stickler for everything being nearly perfect.

3: 169

The first major project that all freshmen had to build was a wooden folding step ladder. That may sound simple, but I assure you it was not. Doc had his four-year program set up on a progressive schedule. Every project led to you being able to build a more complicated project, until you had gained the basic skills he wanted you to graduate with. The program was based heavily on the fabrication of agricultural equipment. Every project had to be started with a mechanical drawing of the item you intended to build. The drawing was drawn to scale, and the wording included had to be in a handwritten font that Doc required. Doc figured if you couldn't draw it, you probably couldn't build it.

Doc wasn't worried about the precious feelings of high school boys. If you did the project according to his specifications, it passed. If it wasn't a quality piece of equipment, he made you fix it, or you failed the project. No exceptions. He hated sloppy work. He was the only man I knew who despised the TV show Dukes of Hazard. It drove him crazy that they crashed so many perfectly good cars making the show. He was a builder and didn't care for demolition.

That old man helped a lot of boys get started into good careers. He could be aggravating at times, because he would nitpick your work to death. Yet if you listened and learned, you'd leave his program with skills other young men didn't have entering the job market. I personally got two good jobs simply because I had taken Agriculture Mechanics in high school. In a world that wants high production and cheap prices, it's good to remember that quality is important in everything we do in life. Building a life worth having requires an insistence on things being done well. We have to be hard on ourselves. A junk mindset leads to a junk life. A quality mindset leads to a quality life. Every farmer knows that high quality equipment, that works when it should and the way it should, makes him money in the long run.

> *"Whatsoever thy hand findeth to do, do it with thy might; for there is no work, nor device, nor knowledge, nor wisdom, in the grave, whither thou goest"* (Ecclesiastes 9:10).

63

Holy Matrimony

"When I was a boy there was group of men who, if they caught a man messing with another man's wife, they dragged him out of the house and beat him with a buggy whip until he promised to be a good boy."

Papaw

Papaw lived in a tight-knit mountain community. He was born in 1928, and the community had some things they took seriously. There were some boundaries you didn't cross, or there would be consequences dished out accordingly. One of the absolute worst things you could do in Appalachia was to mess with another man's wife.

Marriage was considered a God-ordained institution. They called it "holy matrimony" for a reason. The world "holy" means "set apart." When a couple married, they set themselves apart for each other and no one else. Violating marriage vows was horrific. Papaw recalled it this way, *"When I was a boy there was group of men who, if they caught a man messing with another man's wife, they dragged him out of the house and beat him with a buggy whip until he promised to be a good boy."* Some men even got their killing at the hands of an enraged husband.

I'm not suggesting to you, that in modern America, we form religious vigilante committees to police people's personal lives. Neither am I saying the way it was handled back then was Biblical. I share this story with you to show you how far we've changed as a culture regarding the sacred bond of marriage. In Papaw's day, an adulterous scoundrel could get buggy whipped. Now, we take marriage vows so lightly, that violating or breaking those vows barely raises an eyebrow. Marriage doesn't seem to be sacred anymore. We don't need a return to buggy whipping, but we do need a return to God's way of thinking on the sanctity of marriage. Boys need old men to teach them that marriage is sacred and that honorable men don't violate that.

"Thou shalt not commit adultery" (Exodus 20:14).

64

Priorities

"You can go when we get this tobacco cut."
Dad

H ound hunting was my favorite activity as a teenager. We bear hunted in daylight hours, and I coon hunted at night. Most of the coon hunting was done with friends and there was no competition involved. Every so often we'd go to a competition coonhound hunt, where each dog is scored based on established rules. No coons were killed during competition hunts. Those hunts were for points and trophies.

My hunting partner, Chuck Milligan, had a super young Plott female named Spook. She won some really big hunts in her lifetime. I had a big Black & Tan male dog named Jack. He was a nice dog and could hold his own in most company. Chuck and I made plans one weekend to go over near Asheville, NC, to a large coon hunt that raised money for St. Jude's Children's Hospital.

On the day of the hunt, Dad decided it was time to start cutting his tobacco for the year. Tobacco was a cash crop and was financially important to our family in those days. Later the entire family gave up raising and using tobacco, but at the time it was a

175

staple of our lives. Tobacco is sold by the pound and if it isn't cut at the appropriate time, you will lose money. Dad needed my help that day, but I told him I was going to Asheville to a coon hunt. He said, *"You can go when we get this tobacco cut."* That settled that.

Chuck was a farmer and was skilled in cutting tobacco, so he offered to help. We set in early that morning, cutting as quickly as we could. By late afternoon, we were getting close to being done, and we bared down harder to try and finish. Dad commented, "You're like an old mule. The closer you get to the barn the harder you work." Dad didn't dish out compliments often, and that made the day's work worth it.

Life requires priorities. Everybody has priorities; it's just that some people have them upside down. Papaw and Dad always put their work first and their play later. Nobody was paying their way in life, and if they neglected their work, the bank would come for their homes and vehicles. Without work, there'd be no food on the table, and neither of them would've ever taken welfare. The old man enjoyed hunting, fishing and golfing but none of that was happening until his work was done.

"I must work the works of him that sent me, while it is day: the night cometh, when no man can work" (John 9:4).

65

Beagles for Sale

*"There's a man on the phone that
has some beagles for sale."*
Papaw

Papaw was a wise man. He was constantly thinking of ways
to help me develop skills that would help me through life. I
didn't realize a lot of what he did for me until I was an adult. Part
of what he wanted was to instill in me some business sense. He
wanted me to know how to conduct business transactions with
other men.

One Sunday afternoon, he called to me from his bedroom.
Papaw's house had two phones. One phone was in the kitchen,
and the other phone was in the bedroom. To use the phone in the
kitchen, you had to stand up the entire call, so any lengthy calls
were taken in the bedroom, where there was a place to sit. When
I entered the bedroom, he said, *"There's a man on the phone that
has some beagles for sale."* Papaw knew I wanted some beagles to
use for rabbit hunting, so he found some for sale and had already
made the deal. But he wasn't going to miss an opportunity to
teach me in the process.

Papaw had prearranged with the man who owned the beagles to do the deal with me over the phone. It was all planned between the two men, but I didn't know that. I answered the phone and talked through the matter with the man and agreed to buy a pair of male beagles from him. On another occasion, Papaw arranged for me to buy some hogs from a cousin. It was the first time I ever wrote a check to pay for something. Buying, swapping and trading is an important skill set. I'll admit, I'm not the business mind Papaw was, but those lessons in business helped me with the basics.

Boys need to know how to look other men in the eye, make deals and shake hands with a man's handshake. Then they need to follow through on their end of the deal. Fair and honest dealing will give you a good name. Last summer I took my granddaughter to visit a border collie kennel. She had been asking for a border collie, and I wanted a cow dog to use on the farm. We agreed to go into partnership on a puppy. I prearranged with the kennel owner for my 5-year-old granddaughter to do the deal. I was emotional watching her hand him the money as he talked to her like an adult. I was now the proud Papaw.

"And if thou sell ought unto thy neighbour, or buyest ought of thy neighbour's hand, ye shall not oppress one another" (Leviticus 25:14).

66

Focus

"Are you watching for tracks?"
Papaw

W hen you bear hunt with hounds, the first thing you do every morning is look for a fresh bear track. As you drive up mountain roads, the dogs stick their noses out of the dog box and smell for bear scent. The men in the trucks watch on either side of the truck in search of a visible track. In the mountains, you usually have steep banks on both sides of the road. When a bear walks down a bank, he leaves tracks. If you're paying attention, you can spot them.

Before I was old enough to drive, I would sit in the passenger seat of Papaw's truck and look out the window, hoping to be the one who found a good track to run. I'd watch closely for a while, and then I'd get distracted or zoned out. Papaw would say multiple times a morning, *"Are you watching for tracks?"* When he'd catch me zoned out, I'd snap my eyes back into position and start watching intently again.

Driving miles through the forest watching for a track is tedious for a boy. If you look away even for a split second, you can miss out. Focus is essential. Unfortunately, young boys are not running over with focus. It's an acquired discipline over time, developed by people who care enough about something for that something to keep their attention.

The most important things in life require focus. Getting distracted by matters of lesser importance robs us of the best things. Nobody can be great at everything. Whatever you determine you want to be great at will demand your attention. Christians, of all people, ought to understand this principle. We are commanded to keep our eyes on Jesus. If the world distracts us from that, we're going to falter in ways that are exceedingly important. The old man seemed to always know when I wasn't looking.

"Looking unto Jesus the author and finisher of our faith; who for the joy that was set before him endured the cross, despising the shame, and is set down at the right hand of the throne of God" (Hebrews 12:2).

Berry Tarlton with his great grandson Benjamin Jones. Ben killed his first bear this day.

67

Equipment

"You can't kill what you can't see."
Donald "Buck" Sandstrom

O ur family was a hunting family. Mostly, we bear hunted with hounds. Dad and I seldom missed opening day of dove season. Deer hunting was important because we ate a lot of deer meat. Things were kept simple, and the equipment we used was basic. Truthfully, we didn't know much of what was going on in the outside world regarding the latest and greatest in hunting technology. Sometimes, our equipment was woefully inadequate compared to what other people used. If you want an example of inadequate equipment for these mountains, look up Texas Steer boots that were sold at K-mart. They were foot torture. If you looked in our pockets, we may have three different brands of ammo with three different bullet weights for the same rifle.

My understanding of hunting tactics and equipment took a substantial leap forward when I started hunting with my father-in-law Buck. Buck wasn't just a hunter. He was a student of hunting. He learned by trial and error, and he read extensively. I was caught off guard by my lack of knowledge compared to his, especially regarding hunting equipment. In one area, I found out

I knew very little about quality optics. Buck isn't a rich man, so he wasn't buying $5000 binoculars. He was just really good at studying matters and figuring out how to get the best quality for his money.

He helped me get the point when he said, in a discussion about rifle scopes, *"You can't kill what you can't see."* He explained that many shots came just at daylight or just before the end of legal shooting light. When the light is low, a quality optic can make the difference between harvesting a buck or not. Better boots allow you to go farther with more comfort. Superior ammunition kills more efficiently. Quality clothing can keep you in the field when others head for the truck. Equipment matters.

Most of us don't have unlimited budgets, but boys need to be taught that cheaper equipment can be more expensive. You may save some dollars, but you'll waste your life bumbling around with junk. Learning to find quality and value in the same package is a skill. It requires questions and investigation. It also requires some humility to accept advice from others far more knowledgeable. This isn't just true of hunting equipment, it's true about every other area of life requiring any type of equipment. With some exceptions, it's nearly always best to get the best you can afford in tools of any kind. Cheap can be expensive. Quality equipment can make you a living on a job and can save your life in the field.

"A just weight and balance are the LORD'S: all the weights of the bag are his work" (Proverbs 16:11).

68

Persistence Pays

"It takes a lot of boot leather to make a grouse dog."
West Virginia Grouse Hunter

E very type of hunting has its epic moments. The bugling of a bull elk in the high country of Montana during the rut will send chills up your spine. The instant a coon hound first locates the right tree he lets out, what coon hunters call, a "dying ball," and it's marvelous to the ears. It's breathtaking to see the colors of a hooked brook trout flash in the clear waters of a mountain stream. One of my personal favorite experiences as a hunter is to watch a bird dog running full steam ahead when he catches the scent of a game bird. At the very intersection of bird scent, a well-bred El hew pointer will slam on the brakes, stop on a dime and come to a quivering point.

Bird hunting with a good dog is one of my favorite things in the world. Around 1997, I was in the market for a grouse dog which I planned to take with me on our upcoming move to Montana. While visiting my wife's parents in West Virginia, I did some asking around and was told about a grouse hunter who had a top English setter gyp for sale. My father-in-law Buck and I drove across a few counties in the Mountaineer State until we found the grouse hunter way back in the sticks. After some discussion about what I was looking for, he assured me the female for sale would fit the bill for me. We were looking her over when I stroked down her rib cage and felt something "not right." I asked him if she had ever broken a rib. He was shocked that I found that old injury. He wasn't trying to hide anything. The injury was healed and was of no consequence to a potential deal.

We talked long enough for me to become serious about buying his dog, so I asked him what his price was on the dog. As he was walking away from me, without any stuttering or hesitation, he said the price was $5000. He followed up by saying, *"It takes a lot of boot leather to make a grouse dog."* The dog was way out of my price range, but the old grouse hunter is right. In the Appalachian Mountains, grouse are not behind every tree. To find them, you walk countless miles in rugged, nasty, steep terrain. It's hard telling how many times he had hunted all day and not seen a single grouse. It's not an exaggeration to say that men who train hunting dogs in the Appalachians literally wear out boots on a regular basis. The old grouse hunter had time, money and boot leather invested in his dog, and he wasn't giving her away. I don't blame him. The persistence in miles, weather and disappointment it took to make that gyp into a grouse dog deserved to be rewarded.

Lots of men buy a bird dog puppy in hopes of ending up with a high caliber hunting partner. They'll do a little training. Then they'll attempt a little hunting. Then they quit. Sometimes they blame the breeder. Others blame the dog itself. Often the real culprit is that they simply haven't burned enough boot leather. Men who lack persistence accomplish very little in life. They never get to experience the satisfaction of the men who persist until they accomplish something difficult. It reminds me of the old coaching proverb that says, "Winners never quit, and quitters never win." If a boy starts something, he needs to learn to follow it through to the end. Persistence is learned by persisting.

"Therefore, my beloved brethren, be ye stedfast, unmoveable, always abounding in the work of the Lord, forasmuch as ye know that your labour is not in vain in the Lord" (I Corinthians 15:58).

69

A Man's Mind

"You never know what's in a man's mind."
Papaw

Papaw understood human nature. As a constable, he had spent his life chasing down some really wicked men. He'd lived long enough to even see people you would have assumed to be really good folks, do some crazy stuff. People are people, and they all have faults. They all have weaknesses, and even the best of them can go off the deep end.

Papaw wanted me to be able to navigate life with a healthy amount of caution. He wasn't paranoid by any means. In fact, he loved people, and almost everyone who met him loved him. Nobody was any friendlier, but his love of people didn't make him naive. As a law enforcement officer, his life depended on him keeping his wits about him. To drive the point home that people needed to be approached with caution, he would often say, *"You never know what's in a man's mind."*

To live, work and worship with people requires a certain amount of trust, but it doesn't require abandoning common sense. People aren't perfect. They all have a sin nature and a capacity to commit all sorts of evil. What you see is not always what you get. Pure evil can be cloaked behind a pretty face, a warm smile, a firm handshake and flattering words. Then there are those who are genuinely decent people who are pushed, for whatever reason, into actions totally contrary to who they normally are.

Complete, total and unquestioned trust should be reserved for God. God is the only living being that never thinks or acts outside of His character. His word is true, and He'll always be true to His word. What He has been, He is, and He will continue to be. As for man, you just never really know what he's thinking or what he's capable of in just the right or wrong scenario. Loving people with healthy caution is lifesaving. The old man was a wise bird.

"It is better to trust in the LORD than to put confidence in man" (Psalm 118:8).

Berry Tarlton - Constable.

70

Playing Poker

"Your grandpa lost this land playing poker."
Papaw

I n this essay, I will have to be purposefully vague. The story told me by Papaw happened a long time ago, and I just don't know the details of the matter. I wish I did. I should've asked more questions and listened more closely.

If you leave my Papaw's house and head toward Newport, TN, you pass by a community called Del Rio. The drive takes you through a beautiful valley adjacent to the French Broad River. River bottom land is scarce in the mountains. Traditionally, river bottom land was owned only by either the very earliest settlers or the wealthy. River bottom land in the Appalachians is highly coveted.

On several occasions as we passed through that area, and at other random times, Papaw would tell me the story of one of his elders that owned an extensive piece of land on the river near Del Rio. Papaw's family was extremely poor and a relative owning that type of land was not only lucrative in production ability but also prestigious. Unfortunately, the grandpa who owned that land was a scoundrel in his early days. His vices included a love for gambling. *Sadly, he lost that river bottom land playing poker.*

Gambling is a fool's game. The only people making money from gambling are those who own the game. Casino owners set everything up to make themselves rich at some fool's expense. Even the history of those who've won big in state lotteries is riddled with horrific outcomes for the winners. We know the system is rigged, but the desire to get rich quickly without working is a strong pull to some. The gambling industry has an entire science behind bleeding people dry.

Having money isn't a sin. There's nothing wrong with being rich. Several extremely wealthy men in the Bible were God's choice servants. There's a right motive we need to have regarding riches, and there are right methods we need to use to get them. Boys need to know which way is the right way.

"Wealth gotten by vanity shall be diminished: but he that gathereth by labour shall increase" (Proverbs 13:11).

71

Hunting as a Skill

"It's all over."
Dad

I grew up in a family of hunting men. They hunted small game and big game. Everything from squirrel to black bear was pursued, killed and eaten in our clan. After one of us killed a critter, we also processed the meat ourselves. In our home, wild game, along with potatoes and biscuits, was common.

Dad, Papaw and other men taught me how to hunt. I didn't learn sitting in a classroom listening to a lecture. As a kid, I don't remember ever watching a hunting show. I did read periodicals like *American Cooner* and the *National Plott Hound Association Yearbook*. Much of what I was taught was in the wild places with the old men. Probably the best thing they did for me was let me hunt alone. A ten-year-old boy, with a .22 rifle with iron sights, gains a lot of hunting prowess trying to bag squirrels.

Eating meat is good. Eating meat is Biblical. Eating wild meat that you've killed yourself is one of the most satisfying things a man can do on this earth. Obtaining the skill of hunting should be something every boy is encouraged to do. Knowing how to traverse in wild places safely, reading game sign, identifying trees and plants, handling firearms and processing game can do a great deal for a boy mentally, physically and, if taught properly, spiritually.

Dad was a skilled hunter. He killed game and caught fish with regularity. It wasn't a surprise when he came home from a hunt with the game. When we bear hunted, we used walkie-talkies and CB's to communicate. When Dad would be in some deep hole somewhere and kill a bear, he'd call on the radio and speak three simple words. With radio static popping and dogs barking in the background, you could faintly hear Dad say, *"It's all over."*

Terry Jones on his last bear hunt with his grandson Benjamin Jones.

I'm thankful that I've lived long enough now to get that same call from my son. *Hearing my son call out of the same mountains, using the same line of hounds and using the same three words is satisfying.* You know that an important skill has been passed to the next generation through a shared experience, and there's nothing quite like it. All boys should be taught the skill of hunting.

"He was a mighty hunter before the LORD: wherefore it is said, Even as Nimrod the mighty hunter before the LORD" (Genesis 10:9).

Perspective

"Preach to them that are there, because the ones that ain't there can't hear you."
Papaw

Whilst I first started preaching, Papaw traveled with me to other churches. He loved church, and he loved preaching. He especially loved that his grandson was a preacher. I was happy to be serving the Lord, and we had some good times together.

As a preacher, you prefer to have more people than less people in a service. That only makes sense. Your life is being spent trying to reach people for Jesus. If given the choice, I'd rather share the gospel with 100 people than share it with 10. Every soul is individually important, and that's the point in wanting more individuals in a service. The more people who hear the gospel, the better.

At some point in our travels together, I was bemoaning the small size of a crowd where we'd attended. Papaw saw it differently. He said to me, *"Preach to them that are there, because the ones that ain't there can't hear you."* Very early in my ministry,

I was making a mistake. My perspective was out of focus. I was more concerned about the people who weren't in service than those who were in service. If I really wanted my preaching to make a difference, I was going to have to adjust my perspective to see the opportunities provided. The old man saw it rightly.

All of life is this way. It's the glass half full or half empty deal. Because Papaw grew in abject poverty, he didn't have the luxury of complaining about having less than he thought he deserved. Almost anything he earned in life was more than he grew up with. He was a true optimist. His perspective allowed him to see the good side of things when sometimes others didn't. It also made him a man who was thankful. I never heard the man complain about food either. If you put it in front of him, he ate it. People who've went to bed hungry tend to appreciate food, and the food doesn't have to be gourmet.

Berry Tarlton

If a boy is allowed to grow up with a negative perspective, he's going to have unnecessary issues. If he thinks the world is cheating him, he may become bitter. If he thinks he deserves more than comes his way, he may become jealous of others. When someone complained a lot, the old timers called it "poor mouthing." You'll seldom see a poor mouthing person amount to much. They just revel in misery.

Perspective matters. Focusing on the good far outweighs focusing on the bad. Even when something seemingly bad happened, Papaw would refer to Romans 8:28 to make the bad into a positive. He believed God was good, and everything would eventually be for his good as God's child.

"And we know that all things work together for good to them that love God, to them who are the called according to his purpose" (Romans 8:28).

73

Possum Poverty

"When we caught a possum..."
Papaw

The Appalachian Mountains are a beautiful place. If you visit here and spend most of your time in Gatlinburg shopping and playing at Dollywood, you'll never really know the real story of the area. It's a difficult place to make a living for the average person and was even worse during the Great Depression. The mountain folks were tough, frugal, hardworking people, because it was the only way to survive for honest folk.

Papaw's family was so poor that they would catch possums and put them in a pen so they could fatten them up on "mush." Mush was ground corn meal. Once a possum got big enough for a family meal, it would be slaughtered and fixed up for supper. In Appalachia, we eat dinner at noon and supper in the afternoon. To most people, a possum is something they only see on the road dead. Mountain families saw them as needed protein. If that sounds gross to you, you've never been hungry enough. When your stomach begins to eat your backbone, as Mamaw would say, your appetite will broaden your menu options.

Papaw was fifteen years old before he went to town for the first time in his life. That would've been around 1943. They rode a wagon to town pulled by horses. He said it shocked him when he saw Greeneville for the first time, because he thought "town" was one big building. All his life, the only places he had ever shopped were small country stores. To him "town" was just a larger store in the city.

Today, people becoming criminals of all sorts is blamed on poverty. We're told that gang culture, gun violence and the breakdown of families is because those people are poor. *I'm telling you that poverty doesn't turn anybody into a criminal.* Lots of mountain people were extremely poor. Possum Poverty was a normal way of life. The decent folks among them didn't allow poverty to make criminals out of them. America doesn't have a "homeless problem." We have a "workless" problem. Anybody that wants to make a living can!

If you're born into poverty, it's your responsibility to work your way out of it. Period. No excuses. There may be some folks who help you along the way, and that's good, but it's still on your shoulders to remain a decent human being and make something of your life. Don't whine. Don't feel sorry for yourself. Don't sink into the criminal element. Don't cry. Don't quit. Work.

"Love not sleep, lest thou come to poverty;
open thine eyes, and thou shalt be satisfied
with bread" (Proverbs 20:13).

74

Grumpy Old Men

*"Watch what I'm doing and have
ready what I need next."*
Papaw

Papaw and I were building fence one day on the back of his
farm, when I got a good butt chewing that's still fresh in
my mind. He was down on his knees driving fencing staples into
a locust post. Papaw was counting on me to hand him whatever
he needed and to assist as needed. I got distracted and wasn't
paying attention when he needed something, and he snapped,
"Watch what I'm doing and have ready what I need next." That
wasn't a suggestion. It was an order.

Papaw didn't speak sternly very often, but it gets hot in
Tennessee during the summer, and the humidity can take its toll.
Black locust posts are hard, and driving staples into them isn't
easy. Fencing in hot, humid weather can tend to make even a
good-natured man a little grumpy. When I say grumpy, I don't
mean evil. I just mean at times the old men can be real focused
on getting their work done and don't have time for foolishness.
The old men in these moments will not be telling Dad jokes or
having lighthearted conversation.

Sometimes boys need a verbal kick in the pants. Much of life requires focus and seriousness. Joking is fine in its place. Getting work done in harsh weather isn't the place for Wanna-Be standup comedians. Sorting and working cattle can set men on edge too. Cattle can be dangerous. If you act a fool, you can get hurt or get someone else hurt. I warn new people ahead of time, that when they help me with cows to not get their feelings hurt when I bark something at them. I may not have time to be concerned with your sensitivity, if a wild-eyed Charolais momma cow sets to run you down.

When I was growing up, boys understood that getting their behind chewed was part of growing up. We didn't think much of an old man hollering at us. Even if the scolding came with a few well-deserved insults like being called a sissy or lazy. We didn't have a mental health crisis over it. None of us went around whining about grumpy old men. Getting scolded over nonsense was just part of life. Boys need corrected. Boys need scolded. Sometimes it needs to be sharp enough for a boy to change his behavior.

Papaw knew it wouldn't be long before I moved from helping him on the farm to the public job market. In his world, jobs were hard to find and easy to lose, if you didn't perform. He'd warn me about getting fired if I didn't do a good job. Papaw really wasn't a grumpy old man. Most of the time, he was gentle as a lamb. But at certain times in certain situations, he'd set me straight if I needed it. Dad would do the same and so would uncles, older cousins and neighbors. I'm personally thankful for those butt chewings now that I'm old enough to know they helped me. Grumpy old men are some of my favorite people. I've told people that on my tombstone I want John 3:16 on the front, and "Get Off My Lawn" written on the back. *If a boy can't take stern correction, he's too weak to ever be a man.*

"Thou shalt also consider in thine heart, that, as a man chasteneth his son, so the LORD thy God chasteneth thee" (Deuteronomy 8:5).

75

Something or Nothing

"We can do something, or we can do nothing."
Dr. John Halsey (Pastor)

In 1997, I was making plans and preparations to move to Montana and plant a church. Several churches in the east had partnered with me financially to do so. One day, I received a phone call from Dr. John Halsey. Brother Halsey was a retired Baptist pastor who dedicated his retirement years to the work of helping missionaries take the gospel to far north places like Canada and Alaska.

Dr. Halsey wasn't one to waste time or words. When I answered the phone, he got straight to the point. Baptist International Missions had bought a large boat with the idea of having a preacher carry the gospel to the Aleutian Islands off the coast of Alaska. The preacher who had been committed to head the project had unexpectedly passed away, leaving the project on hold. Dr. Halsey, as a representative to Baptist International Missions, called to offer me the opportunity to move to Alaska and captain the boat mission forward.

During the conversation, Dr. Halsey told me that the idea of a boat ministry to the small Aleutian villages had received some criticism. Some pastors in the lower forty-eight thought the villages were too scarcely populated and would never be able to produce full fledge churches of their own. Halsey responded to this criticism by simply saying, *"We can do something, or we can do nothing."*

Dr. Halsey was right. Not every challenge in life can be worked out idealistically. Sometimes we simply must do the best we can and not allow our inability to obtain perfection to keep us from doing anything at all. Life isn't perfect, but doing nothing, when something should be done, is a failure. Do what you can when that's all you can do.

"She hath done what she could: she is come aforehand to anoint my body to the burying" (Mark 14:8).

Pastor John Halsey

Eternal Matters

"Don't sacrifice the eternal on the altar of the temporary."
Dr. Ron Comfort (Evangelist)

There is life after death. Jesus proved that by resurrecting from the dead. Knowing that there is life after death, all of us need to prepare for what the Bible says is coming at that moment.

Life after death is not a complicated subject in the Bible. Since there is no way to address every aspect of it in a brief essay, I'm going to simplify it down to just one thought – *live now for eternity.* An old evangelist friend of mine says it this way, *"Don't sacrifice the eternal on the altar of the temporary."*

Someday, you will stand before God in one of two places. Non-Christians will stand before God at the Great White Throne Judgment. There will be no mercy there. Each person will be made aware of their judgment and be cast into the lake of fire. The only way to prepare for this judgment *is to avoid it.* If you'll trust Jesus Christ as your Savior, you will not go to the Great

White Throne Judgment. If you end up there, it's too late for you! There is no hope left.

Christians will stand before what is called The Judgment Seat of Christ. The Judgment Seat has nothing to do with salvation. Everyone there is already saved. At this judgment, faithful, obedient servants will receive the rewards they earned. Christians who failed to serve the Lord appropriately will suffer loss of rewards. The way a Christian lives matters. God is watching how we live and calculating our rewards or loss of rewards.

Knowing these judgments are waiting for us in the future ought to cause us to live differently. What we do in this life matters in eternity. Boys need to understand this present life isn't just about this present life. God has a will for each person's life. When boys are making decisions, they need to make those decisions in light of eternity. There is more to life than just this present world.

"And whosoever was not found written in the book of life was cast into the lake of fire" (Revelation 20:15).

Getting Done Wrong

"If you do, I'll kill you."
Dad

W hen you hear someone refer to "small town values," they're talking about the good folks in small towns who know and love their neighbors. Yet small towns have their share of crooks, too, especially when money and politics are involved. Our rural county was no exception to having some bad apples in the barrel.

Dad had worked his way up through the ranks of the sheriff's department, and upon the retirement of his boss, he decided to run for the office of sheriff himself. Papaw was well known in the county and would be able to help guide him through the political process. Dad had a good reputation, and he figured it was a real possibility that he could win the office.

During the campaign, a sinister plot was developed to derail Dad's momentum. Papaw learned, through an informant, that someone who desperately wanted Dad to lose was planning to plant drugs on Dad and have him arrested. Papaw told Dad about the plot and offered to handle the matter himself. Dad was so angry about the dirty plan, that he wouldn't allow Papaw to intervene.

He went directly to the person involved and confronted them. He told them he knew of the plan and made them a promise. *He promised that if he was arrested on phony drug charges, he would make bail, and before they could get him into court, he would hunt the man down and kill him.* Dad knew the people plotting against him were serious. This wasn't a game, so he changed the rules on them. The plot was abandoned, and Dad won the office of sheriff. If you think I'm approving of deception and revenge, read on.

Not long after this ordeal, Dad attended a revival meeting and got saved. It changed him. Other people may not have noticed the changes, but as his son, some of the changes were stark to me. It's a long story, but over the next several years, the family watched Dad get done wrong by a lot of folks, including men he considered friends. I never heard him take the extreme measures he once took before he was saved. In fact, the thing I remember him saying most was, "If they can sleep at night, so can I."

In life, you're going to have people do you wrong. How you respond to that will make you or break you. Revenge belongs to God. Bitterness will harden your heart and make you miserable. Forgiveness is the way. Forgiveness means release. Learning to let people loose who have wronged you is better than allowing them to live rent-free in your head. Forgiveness is better than doing something in anger that will put you in a 10x10 cell for 30 years. Boys have got to learn to control their tempers. Dad was certainly capable of violence, but I'm glad I got to see the transformation in his life where he could let go of things that hurt him. The earlier you learn to forgive, the better off your life will be.

"Be ye angry, and sin not: let not the sun go down upon your wrath (Ephesians 4:46).

79

Men Don't Sit Down to Pee

"Men don't sit down to pee."
Dad

Dad had a disease called scleroderma. Scleroderma is called "the disease that turns you to stone". It affects people differently, but basically, it hardness certain organs. One of the things it did to dad was harden his esophagus. In the end, it made it nearly impossible for him to eat, and he slowly starved to death. As a pastor, I'm often around dying people. I've seen folks die a lot of ways. Dad died a long, hard death with a great deal of suffering.

When dad was within just weeks of dying, it became difficult for him to stand up. He was so weak; mom would have to hold him up to go the rest room. In his lifetime, dad was a bull of a man. He was exceptionally strong for his size. Mom suggested to dad that it would be easier for him if he would sit down to use the bathroom. Dad wouldn't do it, because he said, *"Men don't sit down to pee."*

Dad was a man. He grew up with men. His mentors were men. He only respected men that carried themselves like men. All his life he had lived in such a way that the men he respected would respect him. In his mind, sitting down to pee would've been less than manly. He may have lost his health and strength, but he never lost his grit. Dad had lived like a man. There was a certain code to manhood in his generation. He had no intention of dying like anything other than the man he'd always been. A large percentage of boys today are effeminate. They need to look back at previous generations and rediscover manhood from the old men.

"And the angel of the LORD appeared unto him, and said unto him, The LORD is with thee, thou mighty man of valour" (Judges 6:12).

80

Hazel

"Hazel, Hazel."
Papaw

Papaw and his wife Hazel had an old-school, traditional relationship. He was always on the move and away from the house for more hours than not. He'd be off to work at the farm, chasing moonshiners or bear hunting in the woods. Grass didn't grow under Papaw's feet. He provided his family a house, but he didn't sit around in it much. Mamaw was just the opposite. She was nearly always in her house. Her chosen role in life was to be a housewife and take care of her family. She only went to town once a week on Thursdays.

When they met, Papaw was immediately smitten. There's a reason God says it's not good for a man to be alone. He asked her out, but she told him she had a boyfriend. Papaw had the audacity to encourage her to break up with her boyfriend so they could go on a date. Within weeks, she had broken up with the other guy and told a local storekeeper she was going to marry Papaw even before their first date. They married in 1949.

When Papaw came home from work, Mamaw would have his supper ready for him. She'd put it on the table and then, while he ate, she'd go draw his bath water. While he was taking a bath, she'd turn down the covers on his bed and get his pajamas for him. Paw would then watch the news on TV and go to bed. After he went to bed, she would go fix his lunch for the next day and put it in his lunch box. She loved caring for "her man."

Mamaw didn't care for things much, but the one thing she always wanted was a good car. Not every family had a second car back then, and not all women could drive. Mamaw, on the other hand, drove like Richard Petty. Some people laugh about how slow their grandma drives, but mine would scare you. Papaw always made sure she had a new car on a consistent basis. He would've given her the moon, but she didn't want it. She just wanted a good car and lots of shoes, which she had plenty of too.

Papaw and Mamaw were married for sixty-three years. They had both a traditional and a unique relationship. When Papaw died, Mamaw took his picture and laid it in her bed on Papaw's pillow and left it there until the day she died. They knew what it meant to love until death parted them. She was so ingrained in his heart, that he would call out her name, *"Hazel, Hazel,"* for no other reason than just to hear her call back to him.

Boys need to be taught that finding a good wife is the best thing in life aside from God himself. And boys and girls alike need to be taught that loving one another for a lifetime is one of the keys to a happy life. A man without a good woman is almost always going to end up in all sorts of unbiblical behavior. The old man loved his wife, and she loved him back.

"And the LORD God said, it is not good that the man should be alone; I will make him an help meet for him" (Genesis 2:18).

"Whoso findeth a wife findeth a good thing, and obtaineth favour of the LORD" (Proverbs 18:22).

A Young Hazel & Berry Tarlton.

Berry & Hazel in their later years.

TL and Martha Jones on their wedding day.

81

All Grown Up

"If Martha likes you, I trust her judgment."
Donald "Buck" Sandstrom

Having children is a gift from God. In today's culture, too many people view children as a curse instead of a blessing. During most of human history, men wanted a wife and children. Children weren't viewed as a hindrance to their freedom. Their children were their pride and joy.

Once a man is gifted children, he then has the responsibility of raising those children. They need to be taught how to have a relationship with God. Their behavior needs to be molded so they can function properly within the home and later in society. A Dad needs to teach them wisdom and how to think for themselves. A good solid education in the basics is a must, and they need unconditional love from a dad who will be there for them through thick and thin. The unstable world in which we live demands that children have a dad that will also protect them from anything that poses a threat to their well-being. Then somebody's got to put food on the table for them. The list of things children need from their dad is vast.

All these years of loving, providing and protecting are leading to an end goal. The goal of parenting is to help a child become an independent, responsible adult. When that time comes, Dad has to be willing to let go and let the child make their own way in life. That's not easy, but it must be done. Nobody has the right to live their children's lives for them indefinitely.

When I called to ask my wife's dad if I could marry her, we had never talked before. I didn't know him. He didn't know me. In the very first conversation we ever had, I asked him if I could marry his daughter. His response spoke volumes about his understanding of his role as a dad. He simply said, *"If Martha likes you, I trust her judgment."* He knew his daughter. My wife Martha was only nineteen when we married, but she was a full-grown, responsible adult. She loved God, studied her Bible, worked hard and paid her own bills.

She wasn't a gullible teenager at nineteen. She was a mature woman who was ready for a husband, and her dad knew it. Buck knew he didn't have to meet me, because he knew Martha well enough to allow her to make her own decisions. Martha would not have married me without his permission. She honored her dad, and her dad trusted her judgment. That's what's supposed to happen when our kids are all grown up. The joy of parenting is a child becoming an adult, a real adult. When the old man gave me Martha's hand in marriage, it's the best thing I've ever been given, outside of salvation.

> *"And they called Rebekah, and said unto her, Wilt thou go with this man? And she said, I will go" (Genesis 24:58).*

82

My Salvation

"Son, have you ever been saved?"
Pastor Iliff Suggs

A s a freshman in college an unusual thing happened to me. I began thinking about God. The thoughts of hell scared me. The sin I was committing was dragging me under, and I wanted a way out. During my high school years, I had stopped going to church and can only remember thinking about God one time. All of a sudden, I was thinking about spiritual things all the time.

I don't like to mention my past much because I'm ashamed of it. I'll share it here in the hopes it may help someone. On a Sunday night, I was visiting a local fraternity of Agriculture students, and we did a lot of drinking. Stupidly, I drank whiskey until I blacked out. I woke up the next morning in my dorm room. Someone had carried me from the fraternity house to the dormitory. I was sick. Really sick.

I made my way to the dormitory bathroom and hunkered down on my knees and began puking my guts out. Right there someone said to me, "There's got to be more to life than this." By the time

I was eighteen, I had tried everything the world told me was fun. None of it satisfied me. I was miserable, but that question about life got me up off my feet.

My search for help began that day. I went down to the local Christian bookstore and bought a Bible, a poster and bumper sticker. I determined that I'd be a Christian. I hung the poster on the wall of my dorm room, put the bumper sticker on my truck and began reading the Bible. I seemed to do well during the day but when night came, I'd fall back into my sinful ways. I felt worse and worse. No matter how hard I tried, I couldn't be a good Christian.

A few months went by, and I decided to go to church with Papaw again. He had taken me to his church as a boy, and it seemed like a good idea. That day I met the new pastor whose name was Iliff Suggs. Pastor Suggs was an old man but still a fireball of a preacher. After church, when I met him for the first time, he asked me, *"Son, have you ever been saved?"* I told him I hadn't. He simply asked me if I'd like to be saved. I told him I would. The Holy Spirit had brought me to this place, and I was under great conviction. We went back into the church building and knelt at the altar. Pastor Suggs took his Bible and showed me how to be saved.

Salvation was simpler than I knew. I had been trying to make myself a Christian and failed. Works can't save you. Jesus died for our sin. He was buried, and then He rose from the grave. When He died, His blood was shed as a payment for our sins. His resurrection is proof that He's alive and that his sacrifice was accepted. God had brought me to the place of repentance, and I received Christ by faith. Salvation is extended to man by grace. We don't deserve it. We receive it by faith. That's it. My life changed forever. Nothing would ever be the same again. I was the happiest boy who ever lived during those days, just after my salvation. God had given me a reason to live and a Bible to guide me. I was saved !

Dad and Papaw were the two most important old men in my life. Pastor Suggs was a real close third, because he was the first man to ever tell me straight to my face what I needed to hear most. I was lost and on my way to Hell, but the old preacher stood in the way, and God used him to turn my life around. I will never forget seeing him stand in front of the church, with one arm raised, begging lost people to be saved while great big tears streaming down his face. Of all the old men that boys need in their lives, they've got to have at least one old man of God to point them to Jesus. Pastor Iliff died not long after he led me to Christ. I think I may have been the last person he led to the Lord before he went to Heaven. I praise the Lord for him!

"For God so loved the world, that he gave his only begotten Son, that whosoever believeth in him should not perish, but have everlasting life" (John 3:16).

Pastor Iliff Suggs

83

Catching Trout

If you noticed, this essay is the only essay in the book that doesn't have a specific quote by one of the old men. Some things are learned by listening, and some things are learned by watching. As I've said, Dad was a man of few words. He was especially a man of few words when he was trying to hunt and fish.

On a trout stream, he was a master fisherman. Ironically, on a lake or bigger body of water, he was not nearly as effective. But the mountains were his home, and catching trout in cold clear streams was his wheelhouse.

I was just a small boy when he started letting me tag along. He used a spinning reel, and I started off with a Zebco 303 like a lot of rural kids did back then. Verbal communication was very limited. He taught me how to make his secret trout bait, how to tie on a hook and told me to fish upstream. That's about it.

From then on, he fished, and I tried to fish. He was successful, and for some time I was not. The brush and trees along those mountain creeks kept snagging my line when I tried to cast. Dad mostly just kept fishing while I struggled. But I fished long enough that by and by, I became proficient in the trout waters myself. My advancement didn't come from lectures and lessons. I didn't read books on trout fishing. We had no internet. I became a trout fisherman by observing a master class every time I went with Dad.

Just a few months before Dad passed away, we went trout fishing one last time. That day he was so sick that I saw him, from a distance, crawl up the creek bank on his hands and knees just to get back into the road. When we were finished, Dad had caught two trout, and I had caught my limit of seven. It was the first time in my life I had caught more than Dad. As much as I cherish the memory of that last time fishing together, I regret having out-fished him. I guess you could say that was the day Dad passed the family torch off to his son.

Old men are not going to babysit your every move and ambition in life. But if you'll learn to learn through careful observation of old men, you can do just about anything they can do. Watch them.

"And he saith unto them, Follow me, and I will make you fishers of men" (Matthew 4:19).

Terry Jones.
This was the last fishing trip that Dad and I would ever make.

84

Before I Die

"Before I die, there are some things I need to tell you."
Papaw

Throughout my life, Papaw was my go-to man. He was wise. He cared. He listened. He gave thoughtful advice. He supported me in every endeavor. He loved me. I trusted him.

I often felt a sense of dread just knowing that one day he'd be gone, and I'd never be able to talk to him in this world again. That dreaded day became a reality when he was diagnosed with cancer. He was 83 at the diagnosis, and his birthday was only a couple months away in February. He made it to 84, but we all knew that he'd never see another birthday. My time with him was nearly gone.

He caught me off guard during a drive one day. He said, *"I'm dying, and there are some things I need to tell you before I die."* We were driving up the highway through the mountains where he was born and had lived his entire life. It was like he knew this was our last time through that valley together. The conversation was brief but somber. The primary thing he wanted to share with me was, up to then, a secret that he had held for a long time.

He told me the details of a murder that had happened years ago that involved a family member. I was shocked at the revelation. It had been a revenge killing, and the secret had been held until that moment. All parties involved were long dead so there was nothing legally or morally that could be done. I still don't know why he felt the need to tell me.

It's surreal that the last serious thing my Papaw ever said to me was about death. Death is closure in this world. When the old man took his last breath , my heart broke. He had helped guide my path my entire life. Now he was gone. There would be no more conversations. No more advice. I would be left with only the memories of the things we had done together, and the wisdom he had spoken to me.

Listen to the old men while you can. Listen closely. Someday they will speak their last, but if you've truly listened, their words will never leave you. Papaw died when he was 84, so I've chosen to close this book with 84 essays.

"By faith Abel offered unto God a more excellent sacrifice than Cain, by which he obtained witness that he was righteous, God testifying of his gifts: and by it he being dead yet speaketh" (Hebrews 11:4).

A Final Word

Who is a wise man? Someone who makes money? Someone who is famous? Someone who has a million followers on social media? Someone who has written volumes of books? Someone who holds advanced degrees from prestigious universities? Someone who holds lofty positions in religious circles?

This is what Jesus has to say about the question of wise men: *"Therefore whosoever heareth these sayings of mine, and doeth them, I will liken him unto a wise man, which built his house upon a rock" (Matthew 7:24).* Wisdom is hearing and doing the word of Jesus.

All truth is God's truth, and all truth is absolute. *I'm eternally thankful for the old men that shared things with me that helped me along the way.* God often uses old men to pass truth down to boys. Not all old men are equally wise but almost all men will have acquired some truth, some wisdom and some skills. *Ours is to listen for those truths that will shine light on the path before us.*

"The hoary head is a crown of glory, if it be found in the way of righteousness" (Proverbs 16:31).

Pale Horse

Guide
Service

**Black Bear Hunts with Ben Jones
and his famous Houston Valley Plotts**

Call Ben Jones @ 423-552-1784

T.L. JONES
CUSTOM CALLS

"Call 'em, Kill 'em"
visit
www.ladder-tree.com
to order

Made in the USA
Columbia, SC
29 April 2024